NORTH GEORGIA
MOONSHINE

NORTH GEORGIA
MOONSHINE

A History of
the Lovells & Other Liquor Makers

Judith Garrison

AMERICAN PALATE

Published by American Palate
A Division of The History Press
Charleston, SC 29403
www.historypress.net

Front cover, top, far left: Virgil Lovell with his fox hounds near Wilkes Store, Batesville.

First published 2015

Manufactured in the United States

ISBN 978.1.62619.768.8

Library of Congress Control Number: 2015940374

For Len, who hung the moon;
For Bear, who shadowed this process;
For Mari, Logan and Ty, who inspired me;
For Juette and Kimsey, who took me home;
And for better or worse, to the North Georgia mountains for sheltering me.

CONTENTS

Foreword, by Carlene Lovell Holder   9
Acknowledgements   13
Introduction   17

I. THE HILLS OF NORTHEAST GEORGIA   23
  An Unlikely Place   25
  Heading North on the Moonshine Highway 28
  The Road Home: A Narrative   32

II. THE PEOPLE WHO CALL IT HOME   37
  The House That Virgil Built   38
  Woman of the Home   43
  Hawk Eye, Black Angus and Lester Maddox 47
  At First Sight: A Narrative   51

III. MOONSHINE MASTERMIND   53
  Same Recipe Since 1918   54
  Laying the Foundation   58
  The Lovell Brothers   63

IV. BACK AT THE HOUSE   71
  Growing Up Lovell   73
  The Liquor Maker's Daughter   76

Contents

Learning the Signs   80
A Champion's Take: A Narrative   82

V. Lucky at the Shack and on the Road   87
Moonshine Pockets   88
Meanwhile in North Carolina   91

VI. On the Wrong Side of the Law   99
A Love-Hate Relationship   100
Chasing Fruit Jars   103
For Old Times' Sake: A Narrative   106

VII. A Legal Run   109
Did You Dress Him?   110
Coming Full Circle   110
The Business of Whiskey   118
Black Cows on Green Grass: A Narrative   122

Bibliography   127
Index   137
About the Author   141

FOREWORD

I never thought I would go into the family business.

I was born to Carlos and Ruby Lovell in Clarkesville, Georgia, in 1950, and my childhood was admittedly a rather unique one when viewed from the vantage point of the present day. As a daughter of the midcentury South, I grew up in a strict and regimented household, in which my activities were largely determined by my gender. As a girl, I was placed on a track of domestic duties with no career aspirations outside the education field until the right husband happened to show up at my door. Any wild desire to hunt or shoot with the boys was certainly never entertained. Similar to most young women of my generation, my primary adult male role model was my father, and my greatest ambition was to be my *daddy's girl*. However, unlike the other girls' fathers, my daddy was king of the most acclaimed liquor stills in Georgia and soon became one of the biggest bootleggers in the Southeast.

As a result, the dynamics of our family proved especially specific. We did not live in an environment of trust with my father's business practices being so volatile and dangerous. I was constantly steered away and discouraged from making close friends at school or in the community, and thus, I spent the majority of my childhood with no other companions than my blood relatives. In addition to his moonshining, my father also "traded" cattle, and even when I was a little girl, he would bring me on many of these deals. I would bounce in his rickety truck through the speckled woods and bruised hills of Northeast Georgia. I've been told that at the conclusion of these cattle deals, he would often find me curled asleep on the floor of the pickup truck, having pulled the cattle ropes over myself as a makeshift blanket.

In efforts to please my father, I attempted, with rather mixed results, to join the 4-H club at North Habersham High School. At the time, I suppose I simply thought that cattle were the way to his heart. Though my younger brother would eventually assume the mantle when he became old enough to join 4-H himself, I bided my time as the substitute until that day arrived. The most explicit instruction my father gave me as I entered the cattle-showing competitions was that I was *never*, under any circumstances, to turn my steer loose. This tenet magically became my dearest commandment. Honestly, I think I was more afraid of earning my father's displeasure than receiving a well-placed hoof to the face by a bolting bull. Of course, this lesson was learned the hard way, as so many are. To wit, while exhibiting my chosen steer at a competition in Atlanta, an especially wily judge elected to slap my animal across the rump with no warning. To say the steer was a "tad skittish" would be an understatement. I suspect I probably ate my weight in wood shavings as the animal dragged me across the exhibition ring. Still, I never let go.

In many ways, I feel like my relationship with my father operates under a very similar philosophy: never let go, no matter how hard the steer kicks.

Carlos Lovell has admittedly never been a *warm and fuzzy* character. He did not attend school functions, though I imagine his presence at a youth piano recital would have brought little joy for anyone involved. He was never a churchgoer, nor do I anticipate a late-in-the-day conversion any time soon. To this day, he can be as stubborn as a mule and as vulgar as a sailor on leave. That being said, none of these qualities ever prevented him from being the leader of our family and also my hero.

It perhaps should not have been a surprise when his days of bootlegging were compelled to come to a spectacular close. As detailed in this book, you will see my father's journey from illicit distilling into the world of legitimate business. Over these decades, while my father embarked on the next chapter of his rather colorful picaresque life, I moved out of Georgia to Charlotte, North Carolina, with my husband, and we raised our son. All the while, however, I retained close ties to my family in Georgia. Though time passed, little in our relationship changed, and so I'm sure you can imagine my surprise when my father came to me with a rather shocking proposal: he wanted me to join him in starting a craft distillery, returning to the world he'd always loved but, this time, as a fully legal and above-board business.

Foreword

At the time, the proposition felt as inviting as it was absurd. My son had just graduated Princeton University and then dived straight into graduate school. My husband had retired from his company and was investigating new avenues for himself. It seemed like everyone was beginning new chapters, and I, too, was tempted to join the brave new world into which we all seemed to be embarking. However, I knew nothing about the liquor business except what I, as a girl, had gleaned eavesdropping from behind closed doors and peeking out the window in the middle of the dark Georgia night. Admittedly, very little of this even felt applicable to the prospect of birthing a legitimate operation. Suffice it to say, I was about to get a master class in the art of starting a small business.

I soon became intimately acquainted with the finer points of liquor laws and the individual rules of distribution for the myriad states of this great country of ours—I'm sure you won't be surprised to learn that they're *very* intricate. Strangely enough, the greatest lesson I discovered was that my father had become my equal in this territory. We were both as ignorant and clueless about how to tackle this endeavor as the other was. And so we've learned together, and the journey has been a remarkable one. For all the stress and hardship of creating a new business, no matter how remarkable and qualified a product (our whiskey is *exceptional*, trust me), this adventure has been an exhausting one. It has also been stirringly empowering. I never thought I would be guiding my father through the labyrinth of how to begin this operation or assuming my own leadership role in the practices that I'd observed from the shadows for so long.

Young women today might also not fully understand what it means to me to be sitting alongside my father as his professional equal and guide. Such an idea would have been laughable in my childhood, yet here we are. There is no comedian as riotous as time, and I now find myself a virtual expert in the distillery business, right alongside the man who influenced so much of what the landscape of American distilling would become in the 1950s.

The challenges continue to prove arduous, but I never forget the lesson I learned as a girl: never let go, no matter how hard the steer kicks.

It is with great pleasure and excitement that I introduce this book to you. Judy has captured, with great eloquence, empathy and humor, the story of my family over the course of the twentieth century in the South. I am thrilled that this little corner of history can now be shared with new generations, and I hope you find these stories to be entertaining and compelling.

Enjoy this book, and if you find yourself in Georgia and getting thirsty, don't hesitate to seek us out at Ivy Mountain Distillery. We'll have a sample of our finest product waiting for you, and you'll see that history is living on, tucked off the side of a single-lane highway, shrouded in the mountains and thriving as much there as it is in the pages of this very special book.

CARLENE LOVELL HOLDER
The Liquor Maker's Daughter

Carlene Holder was born and raised in Clarkesville, Georgia. After attending Brenau University, she received her master's degree from the University of Georgia and pursued a career in education. She currently is co-owner of Ivy Mountain Distillery, LLC, with her father, Carlos Lovell. She lives with her family in Charlotte, North Carolina.

ACKNOWLEDGEMENTS

B e careful of the dreams you dream, for if the stars align, wishes will come true. And if you're extremely lucky, the wish (and the story) will take you back home. This writing process has been a labor of love, and one I would not have missed for the world. In researching my hometown and interviewing the people who had molded its history, I realized what a solid foundation I had received. A subject I never would have imagined tackling—distilling and the lives of those who did it—battled my Southern Baptist upbringing and values; it became quite a sparring match at times as I confronted morals and justifications opposite of those I had lived daily during my childhood. All these conversations morphed into a rather eye-opening experience.

Storytelling changes listeners and readers and, for that matter, writers, too. At this journey's end, I am different yet quite convinced that the person I have become is exactly who I was meant to be. Writing *North Georgia Moonshine* has been an incredible journey, one that I had no clue would be so exhausting yet rewarding. Not only has my knowledge been "raised to the fourth power," but I have also gathered friends and colleagues along the way.

This is one family's story as told to me by Carlos Lovell, his family and their friends. Some of the names of acquaintances have been changed while the family names have remained true. These stories have been told to the best of my ability.

To the following, I offer my sincerest gratitude:

The descendants of Virgil Lovell, may this book unearth a few forgotten memories and may you never spend as much time apart as you have in the past.

ACKNOWLEDGEMENTS

The Lovell family, including Fred Lovell, Dub Lovell, Peggy Lovell, Ann Vandiver and Martha Bristol, for endless interviews, spontaneous visits and revolving doors. And especially to Geraldine (Judy) Lovell Rea for your accepting nature as well as the recipe for your mama's sweet potato pie. It complements the story perfectly!

Carlene Holder, for your unwavering belief in your story and my ability. Your power to make all things happen is awe-inspiring. Thank you for sharing your family with everyone who will read these pages. Words cannot express how you have influenced me professionally and personally.

Ivy Mountain Distillery, including Mike Yearwood, Sergio Coronilla and Ivy. Keep running.

Junior Johnson and Sarah LeRoy, for issuing an invitation and graciously sharing Junior's story.

Matt McFerron and the Old Pal in Athens, Georgia. Thank you for allowing Ivy Mountain whiskey to be king at happy hour.

Richard Miller in Madison, North Carolina. You trusted a stranger, handed me the photograph and never blinked. Faith is a powerful tool.

Gary Morris in Mount Airy, Georgia. You have great expectations for Mount Airy, and may the fruit of your energies be a tremendous legacy.

George Frizzell and Jason Brady at Hunter Library, Western Carolina University in Cullowhee, North Carolina. Thank you for introducing me to the photography of R.A. Romanes and sticking with me during a cold spell.

Kenny Smiley and *Georgia Connector* magazine, for proving that second chances and hunches make the world extraordinary. Thank you for the original assignment that connected me to Ivy Mountain Distillery and opened up endless possibilities, including this one. Thank you for the freedom you offer. You are family.

Barry Stiles, museum curator at Foxfire Museum in Mountain City, Georgia.

The National Archives at Atlanta in Morrow, Georgia.

Jack Smith, certified specialist of spirits in Atlanta, Georgia.

Jim Harris of the Georgia Distillers Association.

Willam Rager, Clarkesville Library historian. Your love of yesterday is inspiring.

Becky Russell, my cheerleader and proofer, as well as my storyboard savior.

Alyssa Pierce, editor at The History Press. Many thanks for accepting my voice.

Len Garrison, photographer, storyteller, editor and creative inspiration.

And to Carlos Lovell, what a ride, my dear sir. My only regret is that I didn't know you personally all those many years ago. Honestly, I might not

ACKNOWLEDGEMENTS

have liked you back then, and the you that I would have met would most certainly not be the man before me today. So I will consider this your story. Thank you for sharing your memory, your life, your inspiration and your second and final liquor run with me.

INTRODUCTION

His view has not changed in sixty-plus years. Sitting plumb on a four-legged waist-high stool, the elder gentleman balances his weathered frame, studying the crystal clear stream rolling from a sterling spout. He has followed its journey from a ten-foot-high, 175-gallon copper still and now watches it empty into a 3-gallon stainless steel pot. As the pot fills to its brim, he transfers the full container to the right, placing another of the same size underneath the spout. The methodic transition occurs without a single drop of liquid escaping. His attention turns to the full one, scooping a little off the top into a hydrometer and tilting it upward toward the light. He knows the scientific ritual, but he prefers to pay attention to the beading, allowing hefty, plump bubbles to deliver the story of the liquid's strength. When he is satisfied, he pours the sampling back into the full bucket, which he, in turn, dumps into a stainless steel 200-gallon drum, where liquid ripples and shimmers as it dances in the light. Placing the emptied container on the concrete floor within an arm's reach of the stool, he sits back down, and in about six or seven minutes, he will do it all over again. Fixed on the spout once more, his eyes are vigilant as it delivers liquid gold that clocks in at about 130 proof.

This is where I find Carlos Lovell, the liquor maker. This is where I *always* find Carlos Lovell: at the foot of a modern copper still located in his state-of-the-art distillery—a far cry from the undergrowth and thicket he once battled—arms crossed, waiting for the next bucket to fill.

As the opening door produces a solid mechanical sound, Carlos reacts and glances up; he recognizes me and smiles. I take that as a good sign,

Carlos Lovell takes his place at the foot of the still, his self-appointed seat, by 6:30 each morning. *Seeing Southern.*

one of invitation. If he didn't know me, the result would be different. Ever watching the door for movement, he never takes anything or anyone at face value. Call it hard-learned lessons from decades of knowing what a man ought not to do. A man can never be too sure who's on the other side of the door, the ridge, the creek—and for that reason his expression remains resolute, resigned until he can be certain. Certainty is important.

He knows me, and by this time, we are practically family. It took the first five minutes of our first conversation over two years ago for Carlos to learn that my heritage and his were identical. I grew up in his woods, a product of the North Georgia Mountains and the Hill family. I appreciate and understand the stubborn, gritty, backwoods, make-it-yourself-if-you-want-it-or-do-without mentality. "They don't make no better than Kimsey and Virgil," he announces clearly and aggressively. I knew he was right about Kimsey—my daddy—and I suspect he is right, too, about his daddy, Virgil. They lived to survive; people depended on their creativity for longevity. They made it by any means necessary. I knew I couldn't say that about many people, living or dead.

INTRODUCTION

By midmorning, it has already been a long day at Ivy Mountain Distillery in Mount Airy, Georgia. Bright and early, before the rooster even thinks about his succession of morning calls, Carlos leaves the fourteen-thousand-square-foot home that he shares with only his memories and heads south on Highway 197 toward the distillery. After his routine breakfast at Huddle House, he is on his stool by 6:30 a.m., taking his self-assigned spot. The run is beginning. Someone must be there to watch over production, and no one can do it like Carlos—at least, that's what he says.

As always, he is dressed in khakis and a collared shirt, an image far from the stereotypical overall-clad moonshiner that many of his customers and distributors expect to see; in fact, he is nothing like what they expect to see. Other than his hard-as-hell, billy goat–gruff attitude, he is his own definition of a distiller. His usual attire—including only a sports jacket or lightweight coat when the fall mountain air gets too nippy or when company's coming—is respectful of this miraculous second-chance opportunity to do what he loves most. He always sports his signature brown baseball cap, embroidered in lush gold with the Ivy Mountain Distillery logo. In fact, I'm not even sure how much hair he has because I've never seen him without his hat.

I walk toward him and place my hand on his shoulder.

"You're right where I left you," I say rather light-heartedly, knowing that he wouldn't have it any other way.

Carlene, his daughter and business partner, made sure I knew this from the beginning of our work together. "I want to show you daddy's favorite place," she said on my first visit and took my hand and led me to the foot of the still. "He sits right here, every day, watching the liquor come out. It's what he's always loved to do." From a distance, Carlos yelled, "Somebody's gotta pick it up."

"How are you today?" I inquire.

He looks up into my eyes, and with arms crossed tightly across his chest, he mutters in a raspy rather downcast voice, "Aw, all right, I guess."

At eighty-seven, Carlos Lovell should know how he feels. He had to feel an entire lifetime of emotions just shy of his twentieth birthday, and on any given day, he can tell you every one. A man with eight decades under his belt and more stories than most, he finds it harder and harder to summon the specifics. However, once he begins, his memory doesn't let him down. And if his younger brother Fred is around, hold tight, for the descriptions and memories mesh together in one voice as one finishes the other's sentences.

The Lovell history includes dog shows, field trials, Black Angus cattle, nights evading the revenuers and days selling his illegal elixir. This once illegal profession required being harsh and single-minded, knowing when to run and when to hide. Carlos made whiskey, he likes to say. According to him, he was not a moonshiner because he wanted nothing to do with that cliché.

His liquor was not hooch or catdaddy like those peddlers of old trumpeted and certainly not like these modern impostors, with names like Tickle and Digger, who flaunt their boorish backwoods lifestyle and babble in hillbilly speak, for his liquid gold wasn't—and isn't—like the rest. His was not that rotgut, radiator-produced rubbish like others were compelled to produce, the liquid that would just as soon kill you as launch you skyward. Of course, there were runs for which speed reigned over quality, he confessed, but he prided himself most on the runs he made from spent mash as a teenager. Those were runs made from his daddy's whiskey recipe—the sour mash method, the best whiskey that could be made.

Mine was fine stuff, he says. At least, it was in the beginning, when he operated in the shadow of his father, whose recipe he followed religiously. It is the formula that Virgil Lovell swore by all his life. Pure as the spring water that made it sparkle, his whiskey was hailed as some of the best in North Georgia. The trucks and runners navigating beneath a midnight moon long ago, traveling around snaky mountain roads and the Moonshine Highway were all the validation he needed or wanted. His product was in high demand. People across the South and politicians from Atlanta never decreased their orders. Joseph Dabney uncovered in *Mountain Spirits* that "Georgia politicians had loads of Rabun and Habersham Counties corn whiskey delivered to them in the Henry Grady [Hotel in Atlanta] in the 1930s," some of which we can be sure included a Lovell run or two. Army boys on leave trampled off the bus in Clarkesville heading to Virgil Lovell's place, "the only place you can buy liquor fit to drink." He was never one to listen to what other people thought; he never cared for that matter. He knew what was good, and Lovell whiskey was good.

It still is the same recipe, same technique, only today, he uses cutting-edge pots, thumpers, heaters, copper stills and a jim-dandy out in the open in a side-of-the-railroad multimillion-dollar shack. He continues to rely on his old copper funnel—crafted by one of the best still makers in North Georgia, Phil Lovell (no relation, he quickly adds), and one that his brother Fred managed to save from their early production days—and a six-foot-long mash stick made from sour wood and white oak to measure and move the mash. For some things, there's no room for improvement. Instead of his daddy instructing, he has taken over the lead, and he's running it like he did his own operation many years ago when he was only twenty years

The barrel room, stacked with over one thousand barrels in the aging process, at Ivy Mountain Distillery. *Seeing Southern.*

old, now without the looming shadows of haulers' demands and federal revenuers skulking about. His product is a thing of beauty, a symbol of generational pride.

Fred continues to offer technical advice and notable anecdotes regarding the process, and when he visits the distillery, it is in the early morning hours sitting alongside his brother. They sit and talk and remember and let the pungent, earthy aroma of mash and the promise of another run move them along.

Carlos gives his daughter, Carlene, all the glory for dealing with the government and the law, figuring out "how to do this right" so they would not get in trouble. And then there are Mike and Sergio, the muscle behind the toting, mashing, measuring and bottling. Neither knew the "first thing about distilling," claims Carlos, when they arrived on the scene five years ago. Today, "I can leave them alone." For Carlos, that's the hard part.

Carlos rises from his stool, making sure he has time to walk and talk before the next bucket fills. On this day, he and Carlene are heading home, to Batesville and Goshen Valley, to the place where foxhounds, Black Angus cattle and Lovell 'shine were a way of life. It has been longer than he can remember. He instructs Mike to watch the pot, for he will be back shortly.

INTRODUCTION

Walking toward the exit, as sure as magnolia trees blossom in the southern spring, Carlos asks me the same question he has asked every time since our first meeting.

"You got that thing on?" Carlos grunts, referring to my recorder.

"I sure do," I reply not offering an apology or a movement to flip off the switch.

He grunts again. "Well, turn that thing off. I don't remember nothing." Or it might have been, "I lost my memory" or "you gonna burn that" or, my favorite, "throw that damn thing in the trashcan." I've heard them all at one time or another.

I laugh, shake my head and respond as I always have. "Now, Carlos, you want me to get it right, don't you?"

He rolls his eyes as he does much of the time in response to my requests, but he keeps talking. He has known since our first meeting that the recorder will keep going, and so will he. He has a story to tell. Not just his story, but the story of every man—every liquor maker—who followed along the same back road as he, rising in the early morning hours to ignite fires and prep mash so that in the end, he could clothe and feed his family. His life was the carbon copy of others burrowing deep within these mountains, liquor makers like Simmie Free in Dawsonville, Georgia; Buck Carver in Clayton, Georgia; Glenn Johnson in Wilkes County, North Carolina; and even foul-mouthed Popcorn Sutton in Parrottsville, Tennessee.

Their goal was simple. Liquor was necessary. Liquor was a business. Liquor did not define their lives, but it made their lives possible.

Carlos once told me that there "ain't no way to tell it all the way it ought to be told and I ain't got the sense to." So, we decided to let the words of his father pilot the tale. Introducing each chapter are the words of Virgil Lovell—Virge, as he was known to most—seasoned and toughened by the testament of living sixty-eight years, most of them side by side with a hardworking woman, ten bullheaded children, herds of Black Angus cattle, spirited foxhounds and gallons upon gallons of the best 'shine in the North Georgia mountains.

I

THE HILLS OF
NORTHEAST GEORGIA

Little boats stay close to shore; big boats venture forth more.
—Virge Lovell

Never forget where you come from. It is a clear picture of where you will end up.

Northeastern Georgia, the southern section of the Appalachian Mountains, is this story's setting and foundation. In *The Appalachians: America's First and Last Frontier* (edited by Mari-Lynn Evans, Robert Santelli and Holly George Warren), this area is described as one of the few remaining regions in America where people pass through towns and are not deluged with fast-food restaurants, strip malls and Walmarts. "Appalachia, in fact, represents the best of us as a society…a great love of family, strong community ties, a sense that the Golden Rule is how you are supposed to live your life…a quieter, more peaceful place," concludes writer Mari-Lynn Evans. The difference is its past, she contends, and only those who grew up here can fathom its uniqueness. What structures the natives were the generations who came before them. The families, the communitiess, the churches and their belief systems—all have contributed and molded actions of future generations. From children gathering in one-room schoolhouses, young boys plowing mules from sunup to sundown and families ending the day on a front porch swing to matriarchs drying apples on discarded screen doors, simplicity and determination to survive in a poor land constructed this region. These communities were solid circles, living on a seasonal schedule, with very few members traveling from one side of the county to the other; absurd was the idea of traveling statewide or farther. In the fall, hogs were butchered in preparation for winter's stockpile. In the spring, calves appeared as black specks on tender pastures, and haltered mules ahead of plowboys lay rows for dropping seeds. In the summer, baled hay was heaved on horse-drawn wagons and, eventually, flatbed trucks, and with the tasseling of cornstalks, the harvest awaited. It was a way of life from which few deviated.

"Even today," explains writer John Otto in *Hillbilly Culture* in regards to this mysterious heritage, "any mention of the Appalachian mountains conjures up images of 'hillbillies,' log cabins, 'shootin' arns,' 'feudin',' 'moonshine,' revenooers,' and dueling banjos in the popular mind. The southern 'hillbilly' has become a stock character of popular culture, appearing in comic strips, television, fiction and movies." In fact, many writers concede that this somewhat negative reputation of the Appalachian Mountains and its people is "primarily the product of a generation of impressionistic local color and travel writers, beginning in 1873," offers John Williams in *Appalachia: A History*. Impressionistic or not, the writers encountered a colorful population, the likes of whom many had never seen during their travels, and quickly drew conclusions based on a mysterious character. Stereotypes were born, including that of the moonshiner. Bruce Stewart concludes in *Blood in the Hills* that moonshiners "played an important role in the creation of the stereotype, epitomizing a mountain populace that Americans came to fear was a threat to civilization." This stereotype "signified the moonshiners the way smoke signifies fire," notes Elvin Hatch in *The Margins of Civilization*.

Ironically, in addition to threatening a civilization, fear became personal. What most fear is "the notion that there might be a little bit of hillbilly in all of us," surmises writer J.W. Williamson, whose study of Hollywood mountaineers is cited in *Appalachia*. "He's the shadow of our doubt."

From *Li'l Abner* to *The Beverly Hillbillies*, America's perception of the Appalachian people was handed to them via magazines, novels, television sets and movie screens. Most portrayed the warm and fuzzy, poorer-than-dirt people like *Hee Haw*'s Grandpa Jones or *The Andy Griffith Show*'s Andy Taylor, who dished out laughter with a side of life lessons.

And then, there was the banjo. When southern writer James Dickey wrote in his 1970 novel *Deliverance*, "Nobody worth a damn could ever come from such a place," people were astonished. It was a "weekend athlete's nightmare," writes Christopher Lehmann-Haupt in a *New York Times* review in March 1970. "On the theory that a story is an entertaining lie, he has produced a double-clutching whopper," he states. In 1972, Hollywood made it impossible to look away as Dickey's fictional account of, as Dickey puts it, "how decent men kill." The fact that these men get away with it "raises many questions about staying within the law and whether decent people have the right to go outside the law when they're encountering human monsters." Dickey regards his story as simple, one of bad people and the monsters among us. However, adding faces to names and resurrecting the story in Rabun County, Georgia, with banjo-strumming, slow-talking, toothless rapists did more to brandish an alleged character of people than prompt a verdict based on the debatable actions of four men.

The Appalachian people, much like every creature, were a product of their environment. Whether positively or negatively portrayed, factual or fictitious, the two perceptions collided. John Williams describes this juxtaposed civilization:

> *Appalachia is both a real place and a territory of imagination, and that social reality there lends credence to both aspects. If we need the example of the ignoble hillbilly to remind us of where we've been and what we could become, even more do we need the noble mountaineer. Whether fictional like Gertie Nevels or real like Ralph Stanley and Ray Hicks,—or both, like John Henry—the mountaineer reminds us that to be truly civilized people must live in nature, not against it, that expressive culture is not simply the sum of urbane refinement, and that genuine community is purchased through respect. Most of all, the mountaineer reminds us of what we will lose if the consumer culture of advanced industrial capitalism is allowed to wreak its unchecked havoc on the special places of the earth. Appalachia lives on divided in our minds because we need it to.*

An Unlikely Place

Mount Airy, Georgia, where the Lovells make and store their liquid gold, is probably the last place on earth they expected to set up a still. They had been on every mountaintop and holler in Habersham County and many lowlands and creek beds in Rabun, Banks and Jackson Counties, but they had never been here. The southern end of Habersham County and Highway 197 was never on their radar.

Had the stars aligned, the Lovells would have had an impressive production in Clarkesville on the land once owned by Lamartine G. Hardman, governor, doctor and self-proclaimed teetotaler. Now Lovell property, it was the perfect setting: rolling hills covered in springy green grass, perfect for pitching tents, lounging and tasting whiskey on warm summer afternoons, the same setup that wineries herald throughout Georgia and much of the country. Plus, on this land originates a freshwater spring, gushing with crystal water flowing from the Blue Ridge Mountains. The water is their key ingredient, and any Lovell will tell you it is the difference between good whiskey and bad whiskey. It sounded like a good idea when inaugural plans were being made five years back, but rigid liquor laws, no package stores and countless objections from Clarkesville residents and government officials made it impossible. Then, the unthinkable happened. An invitation was issued from the opposite end of the county, and the Lovells packed up their multimillion-dollar enterprise and headed to Mount Airy, Habersham County's stepchild.

One of the last cities to be incorporated in the county, Mount Airy claimed early fame as a summer resort town, boasting two impressive hotels—the Mount Airy, built in 1886, and the stately Monterey, built in 1902—where women carried parasols and men donned seersucker. The city's name designated its physical standing, for it was the highest point on the Richmond and Danville railroad between New York and New Orleans. When train travel decreased, the tourists stopped coming, and the town declined. With the exception of a few structures, churches and the recently named Seventh Heaven House, where Ty Cobb lived during the late 1950s, its history remains in the past tense.

One hardly realizes where Cornelia ends and Mount Airy begins, as there is hardly any notice other than the crimson roadside sign that signals the entrance to Lake Russell, a small patch of water where, on any given day, fishermen linger on the bank. Long gone are the days of resort town status; it's simply the in-between to another destination.

Habersham County historian William Raper remembers it being "one of the worst known towns in the state of Georgia. You could walk out on the porch, and somebody [was as] liable to shoot you as not. It was mean. That town's been mean down through the years. [At] all the beer joints—the Brown Derby, that was the famous one, and there was another one—if you walked in, you better back out. And the bootlegging going on throughout the years, selling liquor out of the back door."

Backdoor days are gone, but even these days, no liquor flows from the Lovells' front or back door. It was only in 2014 that craft distillers could share a scant sample with consumers in their distillery and then only half an ounce per customer per day. In addition, Georgia laws prohibit any product sales from a distillery. With Mount Airy's Puritan reputation, the

Lovells were up against two battles—strict government laws and liquor's previous reputation.

"Mount Airy has always walked to the beat of a different drummer," Carlene remembers, along with the specific instructions she and most of her friends received from the adults to avoid that part of the county. Like many sleepy southern towns these days, economic expansion has eluded Mount Airy; it finds itself attempting to revitalize. Focusing on the positive, government officials are attempting to breathe new life into its future by capitalizing on its past.

Mayor Gary E. Morris acknowledges that his town has "a bad reputation of being the worst north of Phoenix, Alabama. People were afraid to ride through" mainly due to the Brown Derby, the Oasis, the Deluxe Tavern and Fred's Tavern, all located within a stone's throw of one another. A quintessential Saturday night took people from the Derby to the Oasis and then from the Deluxe to Fred's, and by Sunday morning, no one knew where they had been or where they were.

Years back, "someone had crossed the street to go to the other tavern and someone hit him," recalls Morris. He can still see the guy lying with his hind-end in the ditch and his feet on the road, asking, "What'd I fall off?"

Ready to clean up his town, Morris ran for city council in 1982, and with no financial interest in the liquor joints and not being related to those who preceded him in government, he won on the platform of change and cleanup. However, his being in office didn't bring about immediate transformation. Inspections uncovered filthy conditions, stashes of illegal non-taxed liquor and rooms in the back for *tired* hostesses. During one of the final nights at the Brown Derby, a man was shot at its entrance, and there he lay as patrons stepped over him to get a drink. Even the man who shot him sat at the bar. The two had been arguing, and they knew they could finish their spat in Mount Airy; no matter the outcome, nothing ever happened to the guilty here. For the first time, the owner was arrested and a hearing scheduled for what would be the "start of cleaning up Mount Airy." Before the town could shut him down, the owner allegedly burned the Brown Derby to the ground.

"It was a rough and stormy place," confirms Morris. "The people who lived here didn't fear living here. They weren't the troublemakers. It was the people who came here."

Because of its history, Mount Airy, the only wet city in a dry Habersham County, had mixed emotions about allowing Ivy Mountain Distillery to take root here. "It's not our first distillery," chuckles Morris, knowing that most of the community's concern emerged from its checkered and volatile past.

However, officials expect great prosperity from a business of this size. In addition to employing a small workforce, it has brought notoriety to Mount Airy again; only this time, it's positive.

Another positive is the reclamation of the old Mount Airy School. Deemed unsalvageable in recent years, it was rescued from demolition by Morris's vision of restoration. Originally commissioned in 1919, the school opened in 1922 and closed in 1955, leaving behind a neglected property void of tenants. Morris considers it his "pet project" and one that will preserve something positive from the city's past. Although a massive undertaking—it will be a great deal of work to bring the structure up to code—the city and Morris envision great potential.

As new Mount Airy business owners, the Lovells were introduced to the possibility of aiding in the two-story brick schoolhouse's restoration efforts. Renovation would provide a new home for city hall and include conference space. There are even plans for a museum in the future.

"It's a wreck." Carlos speaks his mind and is never short on words or opinions. "It looks good on the outside, but it's a wreck on the inside."

"They're going to put the city council in the bottom, and they wondered…" Carlene begins to explain.

"It's tore up." Carlos cuts her off. "It ain't fit for nothing. If you had all the money we could put in this truck, I wouldn't put it in that building. You can count me out. Not today. Not tomorrow."

"Forget it off your mind, Carlene," bellows Carlos.

"It's not on my mind, Daddy."

"They wanted it as a museum, and they want us to help fix it up," adds Carlos. "I got all I want of Mount Airy right now. We couldn't make any money out there. Tell you what, Carlene. We got to ride our own horse. Let them ride their own horse."

And so it goes. That's how the new kid in town sees it. And that's how it will be.

HEADING NORTH ON THE MOONSHINE HIGHWAY

Past the distillery heading out of Mount Airy is the southern tip of Highway 197, the famous—or infamous, depending on who is spouting the tale—road where history has been made for nearly a century. Some people call it Scenic 197; others, the Moonshine Highway. Unlike its northern apex, where it crosses over into Rabun County and loses itself within the Chattahoochee National Forest, here at its jumping-off point, commotion does not shadow trucks or people. It simply transports people from one end of the county to the other. Head eight miles north, and it evolves from its straight roads lined with flatlands into a totally different character, one that is dangerous, curvy, heavily trafficked and even known to take a life at a moment's notice. Legend has it that bootleggers allegedly used its dangerous curves to "take care of" a federal agent who received word from an informant of a liquor run going down that night. The agent responded and rear-ended a bootlegger's car, which had stalled in the middle of the snaky road; its trunk was filled with dynamite. Even today, simple sightseeing takes concentration and an iron-clad stomach, one not moved by a snaky passage of ins-and-outs flanked by rushing mountain streams and heavily wooded forests, dense as the steamy July heat.

Highway 197 is home for Carlos and has been for most of his life. Neither he nor Carlene can remember the last time they traveled toward the Virgil Lovell homestead in Batesville, a farm that saw the beginnings of twelve lives deeply rooted in family values, hard work and southern tradition. However, they do remember the string of towns and communities in between and their family connections.

Cornelia, the county's largest city, provided the cultural and economic needs for the county's population. It was the place to be fitted for Florsheim shoes, to purchase winter coats at Gold's Department Store and to gather around the railroad depot, Home of the Big Red Apple. Named for the wife of a railroad magnate, Cornelia, like Mount Airy, was a bustling railroad town, where at the turn of the century, German and

Downtown Cornelia, late 1930s. *R.A. Romanes Collection, Western Carolina University.*

President Roosevelt's funeral train near Alto, southern Habersham County. *R.A. Romanes Collection, Western Carolina University.*

Swiss immigrants tried their hands at cotton, timber and even winemaking skills—that is, until Prohibition.

No winemaking or drinking was allowed in the neighboring city of Demorest, for it, according to some New Englanders, was the South's version of Utopia, where the morals would be strictly regulated and education and industry would be its center. Time tested those ideals, and today, the center of town is full of lively Piedmont College students, making those New Englanders' goal for educational prosperity a reality. A touchstone for the Lovell family, the college offered employment for Lillie Lovell and, in 1949, a teaching degree for Ruby, Carlos's wife.

Only a few miles north is Clarkesville, the county seat. It was first the home to Cherokee Indians and later the white man. Like most of the surrounding townships, it was a resort town where people would spend summers traveling from the center of town to Cornelia on streetcars and then, in 1924, on the first paved road north of Atlanta. Once named America's number-one retirement community, it continues to move at a retirement pace, slow and steady, as residents take time to stop and smell the mountain laurel. The downtown square isn't much different than it was in years past. There is no Turpin's Drugstore, Moulders or Kimsey's Motel, but locally owned small businesses like coffee shops and art galleries are still the main presence.

Downtown Clarkesville, late 1930s. *R.A. Romanes Collection, Western Carolina University.*

The Charm House, Clarkesville, late 1930s. *R.A. Romanes Collection, Western Carolina University.*

Beyond the historic town square, a U-shaped curve points in the direction of Highway 197. Its first signature landmark is Bethlehem Baptist Church. Established as the first Southern Baptist church in Georgia and built in 1818, a small white sanctuary was replaced in the early 1970s with a massive contemporary complex. Next, North Georgia Technical School—or the Trade School, as locals call it—appears unchanged with time. Other than the occasional modern glass building and the construction sprawl into what were once baseball fields, Georgia's first vocational school looks as familiar as it did on the days when I pressed my face against the school bus windows. Next was Hardman Road, named for its primary property owner, Lamartine Hardman, who, according to *New Georgia Encyclopedia*, was considered to be "one of the wealthiest men in North Georgia at the turn of the twentieth century." Owning properties in seven Georgia counties, including the bulk of Hardman Road at one time, Lamartine Hardman served in the state legislature from 1902 to 1907 and was elected governor in 1926 at the age of seventy-one. In addition to his extraordinary medical achievements and entrepreneurial pursuits, he was known for introducing in the state legislature the bill to ban the sale of alcohol in Georgia. It passed by an overwhelming margin. Today, Carlos Lovell owns Hardman's property.

A most scenic drive, Highway 197's character extends beyond notables on maps. A stream of water once cascaded over a five-foot lull in the road that suddenly rose and dipped and rose again in the span of a few hundred feet. Famously known to every resident from miles around and labeled as the Dip, it was the spot that defined the road. Every high school senior with his buddies sped up and slammed into those few gallons of water, exhilarated by an adrenalin rush of risk. The water no longer slips over the pavement; a barricade diverts the water underneath the road, abolishing the thrill of ice-cold mountain water splashing through a vehicle's open windows. It was also this very same flow that made the mash, cooled the vapors and condensed mountain 'shine back to liquid for the Lovell brothers during their lucrative 1950s and '60s.

THE ROAD HOME: A NARRATIVE

The drive is as most of us remember—curvy and quick.

"Don't let me throw you around on these curves making you sick," says Carlene, leaning toward the backseat in my direction.

"Aw, you can't make her sick," barks Carlos, riding shotgun. "If we do, we'll let her out and let her get sick and put her back in. Like we did when we's foxhunting. We'd go to the dog show, have the dogs in the car, they'd get sick riding. We'd let 'em get sick in the ditches and put 'em back in the car. Then go back up the road." Without skipping a breath, he looks at the property on the right and asks, "I used to own that, didn't I?"

Foxhounds and field trials were as much a part of Carlos's life as mash and moonshine. Admittedly, unlike liquor, there was no money in dogs, but they added purpose and pride.

His jagged memory appears from out of the blue as his head bobs from the left to the right. We pass his brother Fred's real estate office, a one-room house complete with an upright piano in the sales room. "He still sells property," Carlos confirms as he spots the white Chevy Silverado in the parking area. "Sure enough, there he sits." Farther along the route, he looks left. "That belongs to Ted Turner," he says, bragging that Fred, along with the likes of Jay Leno, is a frequent guest at Turner's yearly birthday party. "He doesn't do anything with it; he just comes to fish." A stretch of pasture catches his eyes. "There's where the old feedlot used to be 'fore we tore it down." We pass Howard Cheek's house, "as good a people as ever was." Then, "Every time I drive up this road, I kick my hind-end for not buying that farm right there. I could've bought it for nothing."

This road works magic. From foxhounds to land deals and good people, Carlos is going home.

"Are you still buying land?" I ask.

"Yes, if the price is right I'll buy it," he responds. As his father believed before him, purchasing land with stockpiled cash meant wealth to Carlos. Whether a man were twenty or eighty-seven, land was a commodity that ensured sustainability. "I bought some of that right there." He points to a green lush pasture, a section overrun with weeds and wielding a crumbling barn. "It was high, but I bought it anyway." He looks toward the other side of the road and gestures. "I could've bought that land right there. It was a whole lot of money at one time, and I should've bought it." There are few regrets he voices.

From cattle farms to chicken houses, the road serves as a barometer of hardworking mountaineers. Each home place tells tales of the history of a breed that appear to be disappearing from the twenty-first-century landscape; nevertheless, it is a history with a stable foundation on which the elder generation clings.

A sudden right-angle turn, followed by a three-way stop, is the first visible sign of entering the county's most northern city, Batesville, a place where locals believed in letting the "sun shine in and the moon shine out," as one resident explained. There are nothing more than a store at the apex of the curve and a few others down the road that substantiate the assemblage of a community. Providence Church and what remains of the Providence School and gym still sit crosswise one hundred yards in the distance. The town's first community school, Providence was built in 1820, according to historian William Raper, and was eventually torn down, being replaced by a four-classroom structure in 1885. Today, all that remains is the gym, which was renovated in 2000 for community use.

Batesville residents are "a breed of people of their own," continues Raper. "Outsiders just don't go to Batesville. It's like a close-knit family. It's even reflected in the elections in the county. If you got the people from Batesville and the people from Demorest to go along with a candidate, nine times out of ten, they would be elected. South of Demorest, very seldom has there ever been a sheriff elected—all come out of the north end of the county. It made a lot of difference. Clarkesville, Demorest, Batesville carried a lot of influence."

Most people who grew up here remained here, as did most who lived deep within secluded mountain hamlets. They were not a transient population.

"All I can say, it's just like the old days," Raper says. "You have a settlement in one area, and they never got out of that area. That's mainly [it] with Batesville. Batesville is Batesville; that's all I can say. It was hard for anyone to infiltrate into this. They were very close-knit about outsiders. You keep it quiet."

Farther north, the Mark of the Potter rests within a few feet of the narrow road. Since 1969, artisans and potters have showcased stoneware of unique interpretations, but long before, it was Watts Grist Mill, the farmers' hub for grinding corn and wheat. The turbine was powered by the majestic Soque River, which still runs beneath the mill and chases the road's path. Some thirty miles long, it is the heartbeat of this highway. Although most of its waters rush through private land, flashes can be seen from the road. It is trapped within Habersham County and empties into the Chattahoochee River at the county's southern end. Tributaries of the Soque River wind down Tray Mountain, the county's tallest peak at 4,430 feet, and descend into Goshen Valley.

At Habersham's most northern point is Lake Burton, a man-made reservoir created from the Tallulah River. It was named for the town of Burton, which now lies underneath the water. Crossing into Rabun County

Watts Grist Mill on Highway 197, Clarkesville, 1937. *R.A. Romanes Collection, Western Carolina University.*

Lake Burton, 1936. *R.A. Romanes Collection, Western Carolina University.*

is the Chattahoochee National Forest, established in 1937, a massive expanse of slopes and ridges, covered with mixed oak and pine timbers, an inviting environment for hikers, nature lovers and moonshine still seekers.

"I've gone up this road a million times in my life. I don't know how many times." Carlos works hard to remember as we pass physical triggers, pastures and farms, many looking desolate and abandoned as age and neglect take their tolls. Others are thriving descendants of favorable times.

"Same old road that's been here ever since before I was born. I remember when it was a dirt road. That's a long time ago."

II

THE PEOPLE WHO
CALL IT HOME

Every dog has his day.
—*Virge Lovell*

I n 1918, Appalachian mountain character was discernible. New Englander
turned southerner Horace Kephart traveled the Appalachians and Blue
Ridge Mountains in the most isolated of backwoods sharing stories of its
inhabitants. What he discovered and documented in *Our Southern Highlanders*
are traits and ways of thinking that are not that dissimilar from those of
living legends found almost a century later:

> *One man will kill another over a pig or panel of fence and he will "come clear"
> in court because every fellow on the jury feels he would have done the same thing
> under similar provocation; yet these very men, vengeful and cruel though they
> are, regard hospitality as a sacred duty…and the bare idea of stealing from a
> stranger would excite their instant loathing or white-hot scorn.*
>
> *Imagine yourself born, bred, circumstanced like him. No arrogance, no
> condescension, but man to man on a footing of equal manliness.*
>
> *Customs and rules of conduct…when you stop at a mountain cabin…you
> are expected to call out* Hello! *until someone comes to inspect you. If you
> [are] armed…remove the cartridges from the gun in your host's presence…The
> hospitality of the backwoods knows no bounds short of sickness in the family
> or downright destitution…simplicity means only a shrewd regard for essentials,
> a rigid exclusion of whatever can be done without…Conversation, with him, is
> a game…highlanders are a sly, suspicious and secretive folk…Primitive society*

is by no means a Utopia or Garden of Eden. As a friend, no one will spring quicker to your aid, reckless of consequences, and fight with you to the last ditch; but fear of betrayal lies at the very bottom of his nature. Casual visitors [learn] *nothing about the true character...until* [they have] *lived with the people.*

From infancy these people have been schooled to dissimulate and hide emotions, and ordinarily their faces are as opaque as those of veteran poker players. Many wear habitually a sullen scowl...and often in the old women, [it] *is sinister and vindictive. The smile of comfortable assurance, the frank eye of good fellowship, are rare indeed.*

Many of the women are pretty in youth; but [after] *hard toil in house and field, early marriage, frequent child-bearing with shockingly poor attention...at thirty or thirty-five a mountain woman is apt to have a worn and faded look...The voices of the highland women, low toned by habit, often are singularly sweet, being pitched in a sad, musical, minor key...The average mountain home is a happy one...there is little worry and less fret.*

It is a patriarchal existence. The man of the house is lord. Whether he shall work or visit or roam the woods with dog and gun is nobody's affair but his own. About family matters he consults with his wife, but in the end his word is law. Mountain women marry early, many of them at fourteen or fifteen, and nearly all before they are twenty. Large families are the rule, seven to ten children...

...The great mass of the mountain people are very like persons of similar station elsewhere, just human, with human frailties, only a little more honest... [They] *have not been hopelessly submerged, have not been driven into desperate war against society. The worst of them still have good traits, strong characters, something responsive to decent treatment. They are kind-hearted, loyal to their friends, quick to help anyone in distress. They know nothing of civilization. They are simply* the unstarted—*and their thews* [physical strength] *are sound.*

THE HOUSE THAT VIRGIL BUILT

Traditions structured the South, and many took place in the local church. Whether it was dinner on the grounds or the annual homecoming celebration that ushered current and past church members home, congregants gathered for spiritual as well as physical nourishment. As certain as a Wednesday followed a Tuesday, people you haven't seen for months suddenly appeared.

Table after table stretched for what seemed like miles as matriarchs' casseroles partnered with the summer bounty of vegetables and paraded before guests. It was here that Virgil Lovell spied Lillie Kastner. She was alone because, as fate would have it, Devero Stewart had stood her up.

Both Virgil and Lillie had spent most of their young lives at the Providence Church and, in fact, didn't live far from each other in Batesville. Each knew of the other, but it was on this occasion that Virgil noticed something special in Lillie that had not caught his eye before. He knew she attended Kelly Mountain School, the only school at that time in these isolated mountains, and that her father ran a gristmill on Raper Creek in Batesville. Virgil had quit school in the third grade, never learning to read or write, and began working on the family farm on Raper Mountain Road just beyond Wikles store. They talked, and he walked her home.

After a brief courtship, they married, both just shy of twenty. With a horse hitched to a wagon that held everything they owned, Virgil and Lillie walked alongside it toward what would be their new home in the Sautee community in White County, some fifteen miles and a mountain away. They stopped briefly for a load of promised straw to stuff the mattress cover that Lillie had stitched before they began their journey.

On June 5, 1918, at the age of twenty-one, Virgil Lovell, listing farming as his occupation, registered for service in World War I and began his service at Camp Gordon near Atlanta, Georgia, as a private in the 330th Infantry. From October 20 until June 18, 1919, he served in France, being honorably discharged on June 22, 1919.

He returned to his bride and their first child, V.L., born while

Virgil Lovell in uniform on his way to France, circa 1918. *Lovell family collection.*

Virgil was in France. He came home to "a wife, a horse, a cow and calf, and not a foot of land," reports Doris Quarles in the *Independent Newspaper*. They returned to Sautee but eventually moved back to Habersham, making a home over Wikles Store in Batesville. As money was saved, they purchased 118 acres of land in Goshen Valley, their promised land. It was a fertile land providing lush flatlands for grazing cattle, terraced hillsides for planting crops, a winding water source from the Soque River and a highland in the middle of it all that provided the perfect locale for the Lovell homestead.

By 1940, an eighteen-room white framed farmhouse, filled with ten children, anchored Virgil's Goshen Valley.

V.L. (1919) was their firstborn, and if he couldn't be found, he was at the creek with a fishing pole in his hand. As the eldest daughter, Lillie Marie (1920), cared for the young ones, cooking and cleaning when her mother had other chores to finish. Irene (1922) followed V.L.'s lead, grabbing a fishing pole and spending every moment outdoors. R.L. (1924) was mean as a junkyard dog, and W.L. "Dub" (1926) loved fishing so much, he became a fish and game warden, practically living at the Georgia capitol. Carlos (1928) was his father's constant companion, as was his younger brother Fred (1929). Legend has it that V.C. (1931) got his name from the side of a V.C. Fertilizer truck; he stayed in school and eventually graduated from the University of Georgia Veterinary School. Earl (1933), like most of the boys, was bullheaded and tough, and Judy (1935) captured her daddy's heart.

With a family to provide for in a region that produced very few jobs or opportunities for income and where poverty was the glaring conclusion, Virgil took matters into his own hands and manufactured his own opportunities.

Southern storyteller Rick Bragg describes the situation like this: "The only thing poverty does is grind down your nerve endings to a point that you can work harder and stoop lower than most people are willing to." Virgil's nerve endings were gone.

Virgil's stern countenance left very little for speculation, and without the necessity of spoken words, the children revered their father. Tall and thick, clad in overalls and called "Big Virge" by his neighbors, he worked the farm from sunup to sundown, plowing fields, gathering crops, overseeing the still and searching for acquisitions of land and Black Angus cows. Only in the event of a church service or funeral did he exchange overalls for a suit; both were finished with his customary Stetson hat. He was happiest when he was with Lillie, often saying that he would have married her when he was fourteen if he had known how wonderful life would be.

R.L. and V.L. Lovell, circa 1928. *Lovell family collection.*

His teachings were simple and deep-rooted, as were those of most patriarchal family leaders in the southern Appalachians. John C. Campbell in *The Southern Highlander* characterizes the Appalachian father as having a dominant trait of "independence raised to the fourth power" and, along with that, independence that comes from a "self-protective attitude" for his own and strangers alike. "He is very emotional, easily moved and easily led by those who have his confidence," Campbell continues, and although there's a disconnect between his religious ideas and ethics, "he feels accountable to a Higher Power for the deeds of his life."

Every Sunday, the entire Lovell family filled two benches at Providence Church. With ten children and long-winded preachers, pillows were necessary, and Lillie made sure she had those under one arm and her Bible under the other. Until Virgil and Lillie's health waned and the children became old enough to make decisions for themselves, they never missed a Sunday.

As Virgil was accountable, so were his children. If he had something to say, he said it, once. If there was nothing to say, he didn't speak. If anyone thought they could run over him, they had better think again. No draconian rules and no complicated instructions were needed; the children learned by example and followed suit. And if for an instant they forgot, "by God, we found out pretty quick." Each morning, Virgil would make his rounds. After hearing one tap on their bedroom doors and a "Breakfast boys," they would immediately stir. There were no second calls.

They lived off the money they made from farming, and when they had a little extra, they saved it. And when it amounted to something, Virgil bought land. Land meant crops and survival and a means to an end. The two-story barn, with stalls large enough to feed fifty cows simultaneously, anchored three silos used for storing silage and foxes. From an early model truck to a modern Chevy, the family always had transportation, but in the end, vehicles meant very little in Batesville, which was at least twenty miles from the nearest city or the cotton mills that offered potential employment. Clarkesville Mill was the closest as well as the first of three textile mills to open within a twenty-mile radius; for the Lovells and their neighbors, those jobs remained elusive. "If you's a good boy," says Fred, "you could get a job at Clarkesville Mill, if you knowed someone who could get you one. There wasn't enough to take care of all of us."

So, as most families in the country did, the Lovells relied on land for income and prosperity. At the end of his life, Virgil had amassed over five hundred acres.

He had a kind heart, a gentle soul and a wide circle of friends. "He'd smile if he'd see something he liked or a pretty dog," says Judy. He treated everyone the same. "He'd just [as] soon cuss you out as anyone else."

Then, there were young boys like twelve-year-old Moon, begging for a wage at Bean Creek in Sautee, the place where day laborers gathered in the early mornings looking for work. He watched Virgil arrive, picking up Mr. Lowry, his farmhand.

"You need any extra help today?" Moon asked eagerly. "I'll go work for you for nothing."

Virgil looked him up and down. "Well come on, we'll pay you something." Moon moved into one of the outbuildings and went home to his family occasionally on a Sunday, but he had become a Lovell. As Kephart declares, "his hospitality…knows no bounds."

Virgil loved westerns and always took Lillie to the Clarkesville Movie House on Saturday night to see the latest show. When his friend Walter Wikle invited Virgil, Lillie and Judy over to watch *The Lone Ranger* on his new black-and-white television, Virgil thought it was something else; he left right then and went to Clarkesville to Habersham Hardware and got his very own television set.

He learned how to write a few years before his death in 1962 by watching Georgia Public Television. His daughter Judy would give him pencil and paper, and she would go off to pick up the fieldworkers. When she'd return, he'd proudly offer, "Here's what I wrote."

For Virgil, life had priorities, which were, in very specific order, "mama, his kids, his dogs and his cows."

Then, there was the moonshine.

Woman of the Home

Even before she met Virgil Lovell, Lillie Kastner was prudent. In 1908, Piedmont College in Demorest needed a biscuit maker. From Batesville, fourteen-year-old Lillie would hitch a ride with a teacher who drove almost twenty-six miles south in a buggy on Sunday night; she would stay the week, make biscuits and return home on Friday.

Like Virgil, she was tall and stout, the clichéd strong, silent type, and she easily assumed her role as woman of the house. To her children and grandchildren, she was outspoken and, like her husband, would tell you how she felt within a matter of seconds. Every day, her familiar cotton dress was layered with an apron and decorated with a rhinestone pin, her reminder of a handmade child's gift found underneath the Christmas tree. And there was always a flowered handkerchief. "It was just like she was dressed to go somewhere every day," Judy recalls. "Every night before she went to bed, she'd take a brush and brush that hair, then plat it and put it up."

John C. Campbell describes women of this generation as having a "stern theology, part mysticism, part fatalism and their deep understanding of life. Patience, endurance and resignation are written in the close-set mouth and the wrinkles in the eyes." In their old age, mountain men and women are given compensation unlike their counterparts in urban areas: "the respect of the younger generation and the dignity of labor achieved." Through their enduring nature and selfless presence, Lillie and her husband remained unified in purpose and revered by their children.

A woman before she ever was a child, Lillie bore ten children in the span of fifteen years while never losing sight of her first priority, her family's well-being. She rose before dawn, making biscuits and cooking country ham—as well as the beginning of all the day's meals—so those who were in the fields before sunrise were fed. If beans, squash, peas or tomatoes needed gathering, she'd hike almost a half mile to the twelve-acre bottoms, and with two sacks tied around her neck and toting two buckets filled with produce, she would return to the house. She appeared more like a covered wagon than a young mother.

Her handiwork covered every bed. She would buy sterile cotton from the drugstore and stuff the covers with it, "as white and as beautiful as could be." And if she had anything left over, she would make filtering cloths to cover the fifty-gallon barrels that held the charcoal for the last stage of the moonshine run. "She did everything she could to make everything run right," remembers Judy.

Butter money was for all the "extras." From her butter, sweet milk and buttermilk sales to store owners, schools and neighbors, she would make income that she saved for emergencies. If she needed to buy a mattress or curtains for the house, butter money provided.

The children made Lillie's deliveries when they were able to drive the truck. "People's looking for that buttermilk and butter," claims Carlos. He did admit that it was a precarious job, for jars of loosely sealed buttermilk would slosh all over the floorboard, making a mess. "But if you didn't deliver the buttermilk, you didn't get to drive the truck."

Each week, she sold to Arrendale's Store in Clarkesville and to Ms. Mary.

"Golly, Ms. Lillie, you've got over a pound and a half of butter, and I'm going to charge [customers] for a pound and a half," Mary said after weighing the blond butter. "I'm going to charge customers for a pound and a half. You need to put more money on your butter." Lillie charged twenty cents for buttermilk, fifty cents for sweet milk and fifty cents for a pound of butter, even if the scale revealed it to be a pound and a half.

"Mary," Lillie spoke sincerely, "when I get up yonder, I don't want a pound of butter staring me in the face. You get whatever you want for it. This is what it is."

Food centered the Lovell home, and it was Lillie's table that brought everyone together. The field hands, the still workers and the family sat together daily. She made enough food for everyone, even those who showed up unexpectedly.

In the spirit of eating dessert first, as a child or as an adult, Dub went straight for the sweet potato pie. Never mind the ham, chicken, roast beef and vegetables on the overflowing table at each meal; the pie was king. Although others begged for Lillie's recipe and daughters attempted the technique, the pie never tasted like Lillie's. Judy recalls, drawing on her memory of standing in the kitchen with her mama, looking over her shoulder:

> *You'd take ten to twelve good-sized sweet potatoes, peel and slice them. If you wanted them round, cut rounds. Put them in a pot and parboil until tender. By that time, you'd have your dough rolled out. In a big pan, she'd put a layer of potatoes, a layer of sugar, a layer of spices (ginger, nutmeg, cinnamon and only a little bit of clove) and a layer of dough. Right on down. Keep going up, up, up. She'd keep stacking it until she got it done, about four or five layers. She could barely lift it. It didn't bend with you. If company was coming, she'd do lattice, but mostly, she'd just roll it out. When she got through, she would take butter and drop butter on top in those holes. When it's come up, she had whipped up something with milk and vanilla, about a cup maybe. She'd pour it on top, let it soak through. Put it back in the oven and man, oh, man.*

Her cooking abilities went far beyond pies, biscuits and cornbread, all the way to mountain eatin' foods like rabbits and turtles. Whatever the kids caught, she cooked. In her later years, her turtle preparation caught the attention of the Foxfire Museum in Clayton, Georgia. She would gladly show the museum how to cook one *if* they would bring one to her. They did, and as she cooked it for the young history students, she described the process.

North Georgia Moonshine

Lillie Lovell prepares turtle, circa 1970s. *The Foxfire Museum and Heritage Center Archives, Mountain City, Georgia.*

Virgil always caught the turtles "'cause they'll bite you." She'd go with him to the chicken house to catch a chicken—"just a small little ol' chicken"—for bait. Once the turtles were caught, she'd clean and prepare them right then, for her preference was freshness. She'd cut the head off first, more often a safety concern than a crucial part of the process. Even after the head is off, "that head'll bite you…yes, sir, the reflexes keep goin'." After the scalding, the scraping and the cutting, she might even keep the breastbone for a souvenir like her father did. "I'd put them on and cook them till they're tender in salt and water," she told Foxfire. "If you want to, you can put a little pod of pepper in. It won't hurt them a bit—gives that whang to them that they ought to have." After the soaking and boiling, she rolled the pieces of meat in cornmeal and black pepper and fried them in grease. An average turtle would feed the family with even a couple of pieces left over.

Most of her hours were spent inside the house, preparing meals and maintaining the home. When needed, she would hoist bags of sugar on Virgil, loading him with 250 pounds: three sacks on his back and one under each arm. Afterward, she'd send him into the woods toward the still.

HAWK EYE, BLACK ANGUS AND LESTER MADDOX

The relationship between a man and his dog is time tested and honored, and it has never been more apparent than in the Lovell home. At any given time, up to forty dogs yelped from the cages behind the house, heralding feeding time. As a member of the North Georgia and State Fox Hunters Association, Virgil traveled the Southeast, showing and winning with the best-behaved hounds in the state. Scattered throughout the house, on every tabletop and cabinet shelf, trophies and platters symbolized first-bench victories and winners at field trials. Considered part of the family, the dogs even had their own cast-iron skillet on a shelf in the kitchen, in easy reach when Lillie mixed up a little extra cornbread for the dogs.

It was nothing for Virgil, Carlos and Judy to drive over three hundred miles to a field trial, from Florida to North Carolina. Granted there was no income in dogs, it was the pride of declaring, "My dogs are best" that proved the motivator for all their fierce competitors.

Carlos said, "There ain't too many people make enough money to feed the dogs let alone all of them young'uns. And how he'd done it all I'd never know."

It was the late 1950s, and South Carolina was where what would be Carlos and Virgil's last dog trial together was located. Virgil was paired with Lemon and Carlos with another show dog. Virgil and Carlos alternated showing Lemon, whose yellow coloring prompted his common name as opposed to his legal one, Dakota Steve. Virgil would have the honors of showing Lemon in South Carolina.

"You going to the trial," asked Virgil.

Carlos nodded his head. "I hate like hell to beat old Lemon."

"You know damn well you can't beat ol' Lemon," Virgil spouted.

"He'll get beat tonight. I hate to do it."

Sure enough, Carlos was on the front bench, having beat Lemon. His goal was "to beat everybody," even his daddy.

When Virgil came home for the last time in December 1963, one of his last foxhounds, Hawk Eye, met the ambulance. "The undertaker come around the house," remembers Judy.

> *Daddy's dog Hawk Eye had missed him being gone. Hawk Eye put his foot on the ambulance and smelled in on it. One of them, Fred or Carlos, said, "Get that dog away from here." I told them, "That dog ain't going nowhere."*

Carlos (first in line) wins the field trial with his dog Lemon. To his back left is his wife, Ruby, and behind her (in the white hat) is Virgil. Circa 1950s. *Lovell family collection.*

They carried Daddy up the steps and in the house. The dog followed him right up the steps and into the living room. That dog ain't never been in that house. He stood there over there beside me while they's setting daddy up in the corner. When they got the casket open, Hawk Eye went over and put his feet up, smelled of Daddy's hands, smelled of his face.

Again, they said, "Get that dog outta here." I said, "Leave that dog alone." That dog come down, went back out the door, down the steps, around the house, out to the kennel. There was about forty foxhounds out there. He went out there and howled for about two or three minutes, just boo-hooing. He was telling the other dogs that the master was gone. You know cars came and went, not a dog opened his mouth the entire time Daddy was in the house. That dog never came back in the house.

After Virgil's death, Judy showed his dog Lady Bird only one time. She got beat; it was a first.

Virgil at home with his foxhound Billy. *Lovell family collection.*

"Lotta people think dogs is just dogs." But the Lovells knew better.

Virgil's love for his dogs took top priority, but his recognition of a good cow and its heritage came next. Virgil's first purchase was land; his second, which introduced the line into Habersham County, was Black Angus cattle. In the early 1940s, Virgil and Lillie became interested in cattle. They traveled to Mountain City, Georgia, in Rabun County and purchased five head of Black Angus cows at $400 each from Blaylock Farms to begin their herd. They became members of the Black Angus Breeders Association in St. Joseph, Missouri. In 1947, they raised the Georgia Reserve Champion Steer. Keeping the lineage strong in Habersham County, by 1958, the herd had grown to seventy cattle and thirty calves. One took top honors as the Grand Champion steer in the East Tennessee Stock Show. Soon, Judy took the reins and showed the cows, impressing local and southern judges on the fine art of raising cattle with excellent genetic makeup. In addition to helping girls in the local 4-H chapter, she helped her niece eleven-year-old Ann show at the Atlanta Stock Show after having won Best Animal at the 1958 Habersham

County Fair competition. Ann had raised the winning fifteen-month-old steer since it was three days old. In 1963, Judy was elected to the American Angus Association in St. Joseph, Missouri.

It wasn't that politics played an important role in their lives, but politicians were never strangers to Lovell land. Every Georgia governor since Herman Talmadge had visited in the Lovell home, and most Dub had taught to fish. In the later years, he brags that even a president—Jimmy Carter—had come around, though Dub didn't particularly care for his brand of politics. Spending much of his life working in politics, Dub's revolving 'shine-making door slammed shut once the other one opened with the Georgia Department of Natural Resources.

In true Lovell style, the children spoke their minds, and Dub cared not if you were the next governor.

"If I didn't like 'em, I'll tell 'em," Dub assures. When Jimmy Carter was campaigning for governor, "he came up here and wanted me to vote for him."

Being true to his word, he told Carter plainly, "I can't vote for you. I've already told the other guy I'm voting for him."

At the Lovell farm, Georgia governor Lester Maddox (far right) and Earl Lovell fish from the wooden bridge where the Soque River flows through the property. *Lovell family collection.*

"I'm going to take your county," Carter says.

"I don't believe you will," responds Dub. "When they swore him in down there, he come out there and I's at the door, and he put his hand on my shoulder. 'Where you wanna be transferred, Dub,' he says. Everybody thought he was going to run me off cause I didn't vote for him. I told him, 'It don't matter, Governor. I got a home, don't owe nobody. I know how to make liquor. I can go back home and do what I do best.' That's the way it went."

"You ain't got nothing to worry about as long as I'm governor," replied Carter.

AT FIRST SIGHT: A NARRATIVE

Twenty-three miles from Clarkesville, Carlos, Carlene and I arrive at Lovell-Wikle Scenic Highway, Georgia Highway 356. Long before it received its official title in 1997, in the late 1950s, the State of Georgia conceived the idea to build a highway from Batesville to Robertstown. The proposed route would transverse the land of the two largest landowners in Batesville, Virgil Lovell and William Wikle. Both Lovell and Wikle donated the necessary rights of way through their properties to establish the much-needed Habersham–White County route. During the official unveiling in July 1997, the families of the late Lovell and Wikle gathered beneath the sign for the road that cut through their properties.

Then, a little farther up the road, we spot a small lane with an official green sign, Virge Lovell Road, and we turn. Due to the overgrown brush and small trees flanking the sparsely graveled road, it is unclear what lies ahead. It leads to Goshen Valley.

Carlos has yet to speak of family at this point in our journey. It's the first time in many years that he's been back to the place where he grew up, and for sure, what he is seeing now is not as he had remembered it. The picture in his mind is very different. He searches for the huge white farmhouse sitting on a crest at the curve of the driveway. It is gone.

"You can't even tell where I was at." Obviously frustrated and disappointed, he jabs his finger toward a small rise in the land where an eighteen-room frame house had stood, now replaced by a small modern structure on the former home's very foundation. No house, no sleeping porches to the side, no front porch spread its width. He looks to his immediate right, to the lowlands. The frame of the barn still stands with its roof somewhat intact and silos erect, but overgrown trees and hedges hinder

The Lovell home, circa 1960s. *Artist Peggy Lovell.*

the view. A fence remains the separation between the bottomlands and the driveway. We continue around the curve, down the graveled road, to a single-lane, rickety wooden bridge sheltering a small tributary of the Soque River. From this bridge's deck timbers, Georgia governor Lester Maddox fished, Dub and Carlos and the entire family taught the little ones how to cast a line and wait patiently for a bite and Lillie gathered vegetables and, securely anchoring them in her apron, struggled back up the hill. Beyond are pastures and cornfields now owned by Virgil Lovell's descendants. However, there remains little visible proof of the patriarch's life along this road, only the green sign at the road's beginning indicating the name of the man who once lived there.

"There wasn't no house, no tree, no road. I couldn't even see the barn. It had all growed up." Carlos finally releases words of disgust. "Somebody ought be shot. It's all together a different day."

III

MOONSHINE MASTERMIND

The early bird catches the worm.
—*Virge Lovell*

The Georgia Temperance Society was in full swing in the mid-1800s, and by the early 1900s, it was flourishing. The New Georgia Encyclopedia notes that evangelical Protestants believed "drink destroyed families and reputations and brought about poverty, disorder and crime." By 1918, the *Clayton Tribune* had proclaimed that "statistics show that whiskey is the cause of 85 percent of all murders and other crimes in Rabun County [Habersham's northern neighbor]." As elsewhere, Georgia's temperance reformers started by "urging individuals to decide voluntarily not to drink and later campaigned to change the laws to restrict and abolish the sale of alcoholic beverages."

The tumultuous ride began in 1907 when state senator and future governor Lamartine Hardman proposed the state's prohibition legislation, "citing on religious objections but also evidence from his knowledge of medicine." The bill made it through the state legislature, ensuring a very dry Georgia beginning on January 1, 1908, and ironically, the beginning of an advantageous future for illegal liquor distillers.

As Georgia, along with thirty-three other states, embraced prohibition that year, long before the ratification of the Eighteenth Amendment in 1919, men's thirst fueled illegal production. In July that same year, the *Washington Post* described schemes to obtain and distribute liquor. Men "carrying two or three short nips in the hollow of each umbrella handle" or women "who increased the symmetry of her figure by strapping around it certain bulbous receptacle[s]…which she sold on the quiet, thus reducing her girth and increasing her wad." With prohibition laws indiscriminant, consumers made bold moves. Prohibition failed in Chattanooga, which became a "wildcat distributing point in the South. A saloon man moved his traps to wet Chattanooga, exiled from a dry Atlanta, and started a distribution agency" that "reached mammoth proportions."

In January 1909, the *Washington Post* echoed its earlier reports and declared, "All records for moonshining have been broken in Georgia during the first year of prohibition." In reports made public by government revenue officers, it is estimated that in six months "10,000 gallons of moonshine whiskey" were produced and "5,000 were captured and 397 distilleries seized." Numbers were not decreasing, and when shacks were taken down, others popped up immediately. The captured whiskey "now lies mellowing in the basement of the Federal building."

Gordon Sawyer in *Northeast Georgia: A History* remarks that in the early 1900s, "an amazing mountain institution, a rather highly respected, illegal industry" was dominating communities. Even in June 1900, an advertisement ran in the Gainesville newspaper the *Eagle*, declaring, "Pure old corn whiskey for family and medicinal uses, at $1.50 per gallon, boxed in plain wooden boxes and shipped as merchandise, so no one will know contents of package." Sawyer points out that the trade seemed to be "okay with local merchants" as long as it was used for specific purposes.

Moonshiners were interchangeable with politicians, community and church leaders. "The revenuers were their opponents," writes Sawyer, "but not their bitter enemies." Businesses profited from their dealings with moonshiners; automobile dealers sold "day trippers" (preferably the 1939 Ford Club coupes); banks, knowing they "never lost money in a moonshiner that made good liquor," loaned monies without question; and lawyers in Gainesville, Georgia, always had clients due to its being the home of the Northeast Georgia Federal Courthouse, where any federal case involving illicit moonshine production landed before a judge.

SAME RECIPE SINCE 1918

Making whiskey has always been a part of Appalachia. To mountain men trying to feed their families, whiskey was money. Tom Robertson, in *The*

Appalachians, explains that "preachers sometimes accepted home-brewed spirits in lieu of a cash tithe for spiritual guidance." For those in isolated, rural areas with little access to towns, "turning fruit or corn into whisky made good economic sense. It increased the value and reduced the weight of produce…it was a lot easier and more profitable to carry a few jugs or barrels of whisky than wagonloads of corn."

During the early years of Prohibition, moonshine produced in the South reached a national market driving revenuers and federals south to seek out illegal distillers. Once federal Prohibition ended in 1933 and the Twenty-first Amendment repealed the Eighteenth, moonshine production was such a routine way of life that it did not make sense to stop. Although the need for illegal liquor was no more, the demand for white lighting still existed; thus, "the number of stills quadrupled and operations grew in size as a result of higher profits. The Southern distilling operations still operated generally like they had before prohibition" according to Burt Johnson in *American Moonshine*.

"Moonshining is due primarily to economic reason," asserts John C. Campbell. "It is, too, an easy way to make money." As a protest against taxation and to those who receive privileges based on wealth, "it is little wonder that moonshining has increased." No matter what, many in these rural areas believed, should not a "poor man…have the same chance as the rich"? When distilled into whiskey, corn garners as much as five times more than a bushel of corn. Campbell continues, "This is a strong argument with poor men having large families."

Of this American story, Charles Thompson Jr. states in *Spirits of Just Men* that "moonshine was the mental and physical salve used to soften their farm's losses. It was also one way of remembering the tastes of home and of forgetting at the same time." He further states that those who turned to liquor production should not be "judged in the context of opportunities" that presented themselves. This salve was considered, as the New Georgia Encyclopedia labels it, a "traditional staple of mountain agriculture."

For whatever reason a man decided to take up whiskey making, one thing remained relatively the same: the recipe for pure whiskey. Grains plus sugars and spring water constructed a recipe that hasn't deviated much in the last century. Although there are some who contest that the means to an end can be traveled on many different roads, authentic Appalachian producers are hands-on in the gathering, sprouting and grinding of the corn. Horace Kephart's account in 1918 describes what many authentic producers today say is the only way to make whiskey, a method that is strikingly similar to that of Ivy Mountain Distillery:

A moonshine still discovered in Habersham County, circa 1931. *R.A. Romanes Collection, Western Carolina University.*

> *It takes two or three men to run a still. It is possible for one man to do the work, on so small a scale as is usually practiced, but it would be a hard task for him; then, too, there are few mountaineers who could individually furnish the capital, small though it may be...*

In choosing a location for their clandestine work, the first essential is running water…the still must be placed several miles away from the residence of anyone who might be liable to turn informer.

In making spirits from corn, the first step is to convert the starch of the grain into sugar. Regular distillers do this in a few hours by using malt, but at the little blockade still a slower process is used, for malt is hard to get. The unground corn is placed in a vessel that has a small hole in the bottom, warm water is poured over the corn and a hot cloth is placed over the top. As water percolates out through the hole, the vessel is replenished with more of the warm liquid. This is continued for two or three days and nights until the corn has put forth sprouts a couple of inches long. The distaste in the germinating seeds has the same chemical effect as malt—the starch is changed to sugar.

The sprouted corn is then dried and ground into meal. This sweet meal is then made into a mush with boiling water, and is [left to] stand two or three days. The "sweet mash" thus made is then broken up, and a little rye malt, similarly prepared in the meantime, is added to it, if rye is procurable. Fermentation begins at once. In large distilleries, yeast is added to hasten fermentation, and the mash can then be used in three or four days…When done, the sugar in what is now "sour mash" has been converted into carbonic acid and alcohol. The resulting liquid is technically called the "wash," but blockaders call it "beer." It is intoxicating, of course, but "sour enough to make a pig squeal."

This beer is then placed in the still, a vessel with a closed head, connected with a spiral tube, the worm. The latter is surrounded by a closed jacket through which cold water is constantly passing. A wood fire is built in the rude furnace under the still; the spirit rises in vapor, along with more or less steam; these vapors are condensed in the cold worm and trickle down into the receiver. The product of this first distillation is a weak and impure liquid, which must be redistilled at a lower temperature to rid it of water and rank oils.

In moonshiners' parlance, the liquor of second distillation is called the "doublings." It is [in] watching and testing the doublings that an accomplished blockader shows his skill, for if distillation be not carried far enough, the resulting spirits will be rank, though weak, and if carried too far, nothing but pure alcohol will result. Regular distillers are assisted at this stage by scientific instruments by which the "proof" is tested; but the maker of "mountain dew" has no other instrument than a small vial, and his testing is done entirely by the "bead" of the liquor, the little iridescent bubbles that rise when the vial is tilted.

The final process is to run the liquor through a rude charcoal filter, to rid it of most of its fusel oil. This having been done, we have moonshine whiskey, uncolored, limpid as water, and ready for immediate consumption.

LAYING THE FOUNDATION

"Whatcha doing home, son?" Virgil asked Carlos in the fall of 1940. It was about dinnertime on the first day of Carlos's seventh grade year.

"I ain't going back. I don't like nothin' about it."

"You gotta go to school," replied Virgil. Listening to his father, Carlos returned but spent a total of only two days in the seventh grade at Providence School in Batesville; he had had enough.

He wanted to make liquor. He wanted to make money.

"You're going to have to earn your keep." Virgil laid the ground rules.

Since Carlos had been old enough to balance a sugar sack on his shoulders, he had been toting and walking ingredients to and from the shacks. "There wasn't no fun about it," he bellows. "I made liquor to make money." Just like his daddy.

It wasn't that Virgil Lovell was a big liquor maker; it's that he was a good liquor maker. "Some people'd make more in one day than he'd make in ten years," according to his son Dub. Supply and demand governed production. And when the demand was high, production and profits soared. He told them, "Boys, if you make liquor and put it in a fifty-gallon barrel and take care of it and don't let the law get it, it's like putting money in the bank."

And so they did. While the activities or procedures in the woods were never discussed, the boys "knowed about it and done everything there is to do. We'd pump liquor, tote liquor, and we'd go hide it." From chicken houses to hay lofts to garages, cases filled with jugs were stacked head high.

To the questions of where to position a still or the recipe for liquor, Carlos responds as his daddy would, "in the woods" and "in my mind," respectively. My inquiries regarding location of stills or ingredients in a run never produced solid answers, even today. In general, as long as there was a stream of fresh water flowing far from civilization and surrounded by towering brush and trees, mountain laurel or rhododendron, the location was an option; Fred quickly reminds me that every mountain or stream in Habersham County, at one time, had a still on it. Never situated near the family home and at no time on your land, a still house was often built on a neighbor's land, just on the other side of your fence. "You'd have to tell them, or they'd tell on you," reminds Dub. A moonshiner would never put a shack on his property, jeopardizing his land and family if his shack was cut down or the producer caught. Ideally, the best tract of land on which to build a still was government property.

The day began early at the shack. Running every day, Virgil hired a group of five or six—"as good as they could be"—to oversee the operation from sunup to sundown. Sometimes, they would stay in the woods for thirty consecutive days, and when they couldn't handle it anymore, they asked for a couple days away.

For the Lovell brothers, they worked on the farm during the day and the still at night, most of the time arriving around 3:00 a.m. For the most part, it was Carlos and Fred who worked the still; occasionally, the others did but rarely. If the run were sold, they'd load the truck "about first dark," and if it weren't sold, they would "pack it in the cornfield or in the barn." They made use of every chicken house, every empty space, sometimes even out in the open, throwing a top, along with weeds and brush, over the cases; in time, foliage and briars would spread and conceal them. They would remain under cover until needed.

Fred remembers the key role his mother played. "If we wasn't going to Goshen, and we had a still close enough to take the breakfast, she'd take a white cotton sack—sugar came in white cotton sacks, just as clean as they could be—she'd take a half gallon of coffee and put it in the middle. Say we had ham or lamb or pork chop, she'd take a biscuit, bigger than anything, and put it around the coffee, and when they got to the shack with it, it'd melt in your mouth." Carlos can still taste "the cornbread, in a big square, two big eggs on it, and a half gallon sweet milk."

With acres and acres of corn growing in the bottoms, some ingredients came easy. Since the girls were never allowed at the still because "daddy was afraid we'd get caught," Judy helped her daddy make the malt. Over the course of days, she would go to the field for the corn. "I'd unload it, put it in a bushel bag and drop it over in the pond below the house. Cover it up with pond water. Daddy said you had to let it stay there for about three days." Then, she would gather the bags and tote them upstairs in the barn "and pour it out on the clean floor. I'd do about six bags at a time. The next day, I'd go up there and stir it, just spread out loose corn. It sprouts out and then stays there for four days. I'd sack it back up."

Sometimes if suspicion was raised, they would grind it at home with the old Farmall tractor in the same way they would grind apples and peaches

Virgil, surrounded by sixty acres of corn on the Lovell farm. *Lovell family collection.*

for brandy, and other times, they would take it to Nora Mill or Watts Mill, depending on who was or was not there. "Daddy would always say, 'You don't know who's watching you.'"

"You cook the corn just like you going to make grits the first time," remembers Dub. "Then you put the water, put malt in, put a little yeast—about a pound to a big box—if you got it, and make it go to work."

Virgil was considered the "money man, the one with connections," according to retired federal agent Charles Weems, who describes the usual liquor maker's production tier in *A Breed Apart.* "Moonshining was run like any other business except it was illegal," Weems states. The chain of command was this: moneyman, two lieutenants (daily supervisors), still hands and haulers. Virgil employed them all.

Virgil hired many men and women from surrounding communities as supervisors and still hands. He employed three who lived with the Lovell family—Lawrence, Homer and Jesse—but it was Jesse who became part of the family, mainly due to his work ethic and allegiance. In addition to helping with Virgil's still house, each ran his own still within proximity to one another—same setup, different holler. The liquor haulers would come through at night, and it didn't make any difference whose time it was to load first, Virgil would call them one by one until someone got up. "If it was Lawrence, they call him," remembers Carlos. "If it was Homer, they call him. If it was rainy and cold, they wouldn't get up." But every time Virgil would knock on Jesse's door, it was 'What do you need Mr. Virge?'" Loyalty was paramount.

"The man down there needs to see you," Virgil responded. Jesse rose without further nudging, every time. He would meet the hauler and sell him his liquor. He made more money and made it faster because he was willing to do whatever, whenever it had to be done.

"I'd see daddy plow a twelve-acre field," remembers Fred, "with a horse, not a mule." Jesse stirred the beer one morning, and as he headed back to the house, he veered off toward the field where Virgil was plowing. "Jesse wouldn't wait till he got to the end [of a row], he'd meet him in the middle of the field and take the plow from him. 'Mr. Virge, I'll take the reins now.' He was a good man." He

Left to right: V.L. Lovell, Homer Gregg and Jesse Lloyd Williams on the Lovell farm. *Lovell family collection.*

Unidentified farmer in Habersham County, circa 1930s. *R.A. Romanes Collection, Western Carolina University.*

began working for Virgil in 1928 when he was only fifteen years old. "Daddy raised him until he got married and left."

Production meant nothing without customers, of which, for the Lovells, there were two kinds: one for the butter and buttermilk and one for the liquor. Needless to say, liquor proved more lucrative. They sold it in any combination people requested, many times at five dollars a gallon jar, with only two exceptions for sales: no pints and no drunks.

One regular customer who was a school principal from Rabun County would buy a case every week or so. He'd have his list of people wanting their jars, and he'd quickly add, "I want y'all to know, I ain't giving it to the school kids and I ain't drinking all of this myself." To which Virgil commented, "Son, if you drinked all that you wouldn't be in the schoolroom come Monday morning."

From Judy's observations of those who came and went, there were four types of customers: preachers, lawyers, doctors and schoolteachers.

Whether they arrived for Lillie's butter or Virgil's liquor, the ordering process remained consistent. Within the conversation of farming habits and family health, orders were made and then the signal given. Virgil would raise fingers—one, two, three, four—and Judy would retrieve the order from Lillie's chifforobe, where boards were stacked to hide the few cases they risked inside the house, and from the kitchen, where the dairy remained chilled. Customers would pay Virgil and say their goodbyes, the order—butter and buttermilk stacked on top of however many cases of liquor ordered—would be at the end of the hall and "out the door they'd go."

Carlos and Fred worked alongside their father until their later teenage years. By the time they were both seventeen, they were running their own shack and developing their own reputation. Carlos knew that when you were "raised to do something all your life, and the man that raised you done pretty good," doing the same was a logical succession. It was all he knew, and it was time to branch out.

THE LOVELL BROTHERS

Newly married in the winter of 1949, Carlos had $200 to his name. His bride, Ruby, having recently graduated from Piedmont College, taught school at a wage of $75 a month. He and Ruby lived with her parents, the Wilbanks, and the understanding was that Ruby would continue to teach and Carlos would take care of the farm, mules and garden.

"I showed myself one day," he recalls. "You couldn't do nothing with Mr. Wilbanks that he wouldn't get on me for doing something wrong. I was digging holes, and he was dropping taters. There was a water spigot at the house, and he wanted me to carry water from the branch to water those tater slips. Stingy ol' devil. I was tired of him bossing me around. I throwed them buckets down and told him if he wanted it, he could get it his damn self. I left. I moved out.

"I had a good place to live, food to eat," voices Carlos regretfully. He thought he knew everything. "Mr. Wilbanks was good to me."

He scrounged up enough money to move into the Batesville store, where he and Ruby would live while they ran the store. He fixed a "little square room in the back. She about killed me, but she went with me."

With the store's income being slight, increased liquor production solved his worry. Carlos told his daddy he was going to take an old boiler from his daddy's place, move it below the house and put it up. "You know that won't work," said Virgil. "You know you'll be put in jail you put up something that close to your house."

In true Carlos fashion, he responded, "I just as soon be in jail as be broke."

Sure enough, Carlos erected the boiler close to his home but not on his land. His still hand Clifford lived in the basement. With barely enough money to buy meal for mash, Carlos managed sugar and meal on credit. Every morning, before the light of day, around 4:00 a.m., Carlos would knock on the basement door, much like his daddy had done with him. Never responding with a sound of acknowledgement, Clifford would slip out the back door and head to the still and start the fire. (Fires started in the early morning hour produced little smoke by sunup.) Around 8:30 a.m., with breakfast in hand, Carlos came to help run the sugar.

Very soon, Carlos noticed he'd "make a dollar a sack on sugar, this and that. Doin' pretty good, buying some cows and hogs along. Bootlegging a little, selling a little liquor." Then, he remembered life getting a little better, a little easier. "First thing I knowed, I had a few hundred dollar bills in my pocket book." Every time he accumulated extra money, he'd buy every piece of land he could. With land acquisitions growing, it was time to raise the stakes.

Carlos's most productive time came once he moved into his red brick home on the edge of Highway 197, just this side of Alley's Chapel Church around the mid-1950s. His father, only a few miles up the road, helped in any way he could, but once the boys were on their own, he let them go about it their own way. By this time, Virgil's hands-on attention was over.

Both Carlos and Fred used the same recipe as their father used, and it was always sour mash liquor—that is, when they produced quality liquor. This process used material from an older batch of mash (previously fermented that still contains live yeast) to start the fermentation in the current batch. This fermentation process improves the consistency and quality of liquor. The remaining spent mash was discarded, most often as feed for livestock.

Although the sour mash process produces excellent whiskey, this process takes time and patience. Purposeful deviation, in most instances, produces large quantities of basic moonshiner sugar liquor in half the time. Fred remembered some producers would "cook the mashes, then run it about six or seven times and never put a bit of meal in it. Just make it out of sugar, sugar liquor, not a sour mash liquor. It was cheaper, but meal was cheap then, but it still cost about $2.50 a bushel." Then, there were the other shortcuts, like using "hog shorts—wheat bran, what they'd sweep off the floor when they were grinding, what was left over. It made cheap liquor, bad liquor. They were just too lazy to make it right."

There was also beading oil, which created the illusion of fine whiskey. Beading oil was purchased by the gallon—around $200 a container in 1950 and only available in Atlanta—so it was not cheap. "It turned blue and would bead," says Dub, "and make it look like it was good liquor. Daddy didn't want nothing to do with it. Everyone was using it when I came out of the army."

Even Carlos and Fred bragged about how much they could make off so much sugar when they added beading oil, and then one customer complained.

"Mr. Virge, this liquor here," a regular customer told Virgil of the cases he had just bought from Carlos and Fred. "We can't use it." Virgil shook the jar, and immediately recognized the beading oil rising to the top.

"If you get caught," Virgil turned to his two sons, "you ought not be put in jail. You ought to be put under for making such rot gut as this. If you can't make it good enough to drink, don't make it." Although the Lovell brothers prided themselves on knowing how to produce quality liquor, circumstances often called for speed and volume, which trumped quality in those days.

Occasionally, they would not run every day, but on the average daily run, they produced thirty-five to forty (around 240 gallons) cases of 90 proof liquor, sometimes more. But the days were still long and tiresome with prime production being from June until October. It coincided with the corn harvest and full leaf cover. In December, when weather became colder and the risk became greater, they would cut the proof to 80, extending the life of a run.

"There was nothing for us to have two thousand cases of liquor piled around in the corn fields when you couldn't sell it," says Carlos. "We wouldn't stop just because we couldn't sell it. It was the same as money in the bank."

And being in the woods, "you had to keep your horrors," says Fred. "In the woods, you had to slip and do everything because of the law. Sometimes you had to tote it [sugar] a half a mile. We'd put a shack up, and if we got cut down, we'd go back the next day and put one somewhere's else. Sometimes we went back to the same place."

He remembers working with Mr. Homer when an airplane flew overhead. "We's at the still and we grabbed the cap off and took off and run as far as we could and hide it. The airplane saw us running and circled. We just kept going farther from the road and got lost in the thicket, but they still rode the roads trying to find us."

Once located in a pine thicket, their shack was grounded to a "little old gasoline pump" they used for cooling. "If we had any sense, we could have run water out of the branch." Dynamite Ellison—a still worker who would cuss if the wind was blowing a certain way—was with them. "He's lazy about toting stuff," says Fred "I'd put a case under each arm and go nearly to the road with it, where you couldn't see it from the road." When Carlos arrived, they had to have the liquor there ready to be loaded once they unloaded the sugar and meal. Old man Frank, another still hand, stood watch on the hill.

"Frank, listen," said Carlos as he got out of the truck. "I hear something."

"That's my little pig up in there in the leaves," responded Frank half-heartedly. "You'll think damn leaves." Carlos had an uneasy feeling.

Just like that, lights illuminated the sky. There must have been fifteen lawmen there, "so I just throwed down whatever I had," says Fred.

I went back toward the shack. They throwed the light, and you couldn't hardly see. But I knew where the trail was. I was running it wide open. You had to cross two little ol' branches. There was a board, they was pretty wide. If you hit it, it'd spring you up. I hit that thing in the middle, and when I did, just as I hit, I went up in the air and flashlights come up. I went over that guy. Them guys run me all the way up the field, but I seen where the opening at the creek bank. They was running me—one or two behind me—trying to blind me.

I outrun those rascals. When I got to the creek bank on the other side, you ain't never seen thorns and briars like was there. When I got to it, I knew they wouldn't go through it. I just shot through it, just as far as I could go. When I came out on the other side, I kept pulling them bushes, going up the hill. They never did come through that thicket. I didn't have a rag on me. Everything was torn off.

Carlos jumped off the back of the truck and ran down the road and up the bank. "Nary a one of them run him. They caught Dynamite for he was standing right there, and I could hear him cussing. I bet he started drinking. He always started drinking when he got caught."

From Kelly Mountain to Tray Mountain, and every holler and creek in between, stills were put up and cut down. Fred tried his hand for a short while in White County; he found it harder because "the law had got so bad. We went over there in a hornet's nest, sort of." Fred and Carlos continued as a team at various sites, and every now and then, their brother V.L. joined in.

"Me and V.L. made a little liquor together, but not much." Carlos remembers it not selling as well in the summertime as it did in the wintertime.

It'd go up to sixteen or eighteen dollars in the summer, and it was twenty-two dollars in the winter when it got scarce and the airplanes went to flying. Bill Howard was hauling our liquor from Toccoa, and I told V, I says, "I believe we need to go up on our liquor. Liquor is twenty-two dollars a case." V says, "I ain't going up on Bill Howard. Bill buys our liquor at seventeen dollars in the summertime, and by God, he can buy it for seventeen dollars in the wintertime."

Batesville near Tray Mountain, circle 1930s. *R.A. Romanes Collection, Western Carolina University.*

The consensus among most moonshiners and even their neighbors was that everyone in the community was involved in making whiskey, no matter if they owned up to it or not. "Everybody did it" was the carbon answer. Whether a storeowner who sold Atlas jars by the cases or millers at Nora Mill and Watts Mill grinding corn or barley by the sack full, you were, in part, a moonshiner or, at the very least, an accessory.

From attorneys to law enforcement, everyone benefited from this moneymaking enterprise. Jo Whited in *Habersham County Georgia: A Pictorial History* tells the story of Habersham County attorney Jack Ellard and how he made most of his money representing bootleggers in the 1930s and 1940s:

> *I did all kinds of work. The economy of the country back then was bootlegging and sawmilling. The bootleggers would get caught, and if they didn't have any money to pay their fine, they'd get up a little money to pay their lawyer and to get the case continued 'til the next term. With this extra time they could make enough money to plead guilty and pay their fine. Our clients often paid in cash from their bootlegging proceeds. A lot of folks paid in vegetables or country ham. I liked it that way. Occasionally the federal*

people would get up in there and send them to the penitentiary for a while. This I wouldn't swear to, but the local law wouldn't arrest them; they'd leave them alone. We had one family here that made liquor, the old man did all his life. Everybody knew it, even the Sheriff. I've bought liquor from him myself. He was so blooming honest you could go up there and buy some liquor and he'd say I've got some but you don't want it; it ain't any good. You'd go back the next time and he'd say I got some good liquor and sell you some. He'd sell that mean, sorry stuff to bootleggers who'd take it off to Atlanta to sell it. Everybody knew it and they never did catch him. In those days if a fellow got drunk in town, they would take him home instead of taking him to jail.

Moonshiners must have confidants and be resourceful. Purchases of mass quantities of sugar from local stores or even across state lines were a telltale sign of illegal liquor production. With corn the easy acquisition, ingenuity was required for sugar.

It was a friend of a friend of a brother who knew someone who worked at Dixie Crystals in Savannah, and there was a truckload heading north toward Fred and Carlos. The brothers were concerned about the driver's ability to recognize where he would unload; for that reason, they met him "down at the white spot." Carlos told Fred to get in the truck and drive.

"Carl, I ain't never drove a truck like that." The only one he had driven that was remotely close was his daddy's '57 Ford truck that wasn't even supposed to be on the highway, had a tarp on top and was as big as they made them back then.

"You can drive that truck." Carlos jumped in the passenger side.

Fred got in that truck and started off. "It started—awawawawaw," he mutters. "I finally got out of Cornelia and made it past Bethlehem Church. I thought that thing was going to choke down. I had it down to the floorboard. It started to rain a little bit, so we were going to unload in Carlos's basement.

"I don't think I can back that thing up down there," said Fred, worried about the small passageway to the basement.

With Carlos on the grass, he directed. "Aw, come on back."

They unloaded all night and finally finished about two hours before daylight.

They recalled a guy in Atlanta who lived off Fourteenth Street who bought a house with a big basement. He parked "three or four cars in there and a big ole truck." It was a tanker truck like one used for hauling oil, and once open, it was hollow, big enough for a hundred plus cases of liquor. "We got to loadin' that thing," remembers Fred, "and it would take all night to load it. We'd cut the case in two and slide them in there." Careful whom he told and whom he allowed to come within, the man only favored Fred and Carlos to load their own cases. Eventually, the federals caught the truck. The informant was the man's sister-in-law who was dating a state patrol.

"It's always something like that," says Fred.

When supplies became scarce, suppliers took notice. "George Goins had a store," remembers Fred, "and one day, sugar got to where it was hard to buy, hard to find. You used to just go up to the store and buy it. He told me he could get two hundred sacks of sugar and asked if I thought I could use it. 'Just go ahead, and I'll put it in the barn. Then order two hundred more.'" Everyone looked out for the one another.

For the moonshiner, there were two kinds of customers: those you knew and those you did not know. "We knew 'em all." And if Carlos didn't know them, "you'd look the other way." When dealing with strangers, the risk of someone being an undercover revenuer outweighed making money every time. For that reason, moonshiners had to know with whom they were dealing.

"If you thought he was the law or undercover," says Fred, "you didn't have any."

One time, a stranger showed up stating that a "friend" in Rabun County had bought cases. Fred thought about it and conceded to having some. Then, upon closer thought and weighing the danger, his mind changed. "I did have some, but I don't got none now."

IV
BACK AT THE HOUSE

You take care of your little red wagon, and I'll take care of mine.
—Virge Lovell

Make no mistake, the Lovell family had a reputation—as did every liquor maker, every man and woman in the mountains who chose to do things a little differently than their neighbor—a reputation that was countywide and state deep. If a person happened to be part of their inner circle, determining fact from fiction was easy. Those who were merely observers made assumptions based on their preconceived notions rather than facts.

"I figured I had a good reputation as anybody did," says Carlos. "I paid my bills, had money in my pocket. Didn't nobody say much about liquor."

Everybody who made liquor had a reputation; some just had a better one than others.

Even family worried about the fallout from gossip and a sordid reputation.

"Carlos, you got to quit makin' liquor," pleaded his sister-in-law. She taught school and dropped by each morning to pick up Carlene and her brother. "All those people in the school know you foolin' with liquor. Those kids gonna be ruint."

"You go plow your own mule," demanded Carlos. "You and no one else going to tell me what to do."

The next morning—in fact, every morning—held the same conversation. Finally, Carlos decided he had had enough, and he would approach it differently. The next day, she stepped into the living room and said, "Carlos,

Carlos with Billy on the Lovell farm. *Lovell family collection.*

I'm going to tell you what I'm going to do. I'll give you half of what I make if you stop foolin' with liquor."

Carlos opened the drawer in the table that sat beside his recliner. "Lady, I doubt you make as much as [is] in this drawer." He paused. "How big is your safety deposit box?"

"Why Carlos?"

He reached into the drawer, withdrawing a couple rolled up wrinkled brown grocery sacks. "I want you to put a little money in there. There's too much in the house." He handed the pair of wrinkled sacks to her, and she put them in her pocketbook. Like Carlos instructed, she took them to the bank.

One morning, she said, "Carlos, I can't sleep at night. If someone checks my safety deposit box, no telling what they'd do to me."

Realizing he had made his point that it was better if she minded her own business, he told her to "go by there on the way home from school this evening and bring them home." She confessed to Carlos that she had wrapped them over and over again with more paper, and now, she could not get them all in her pocketbook at once, that it would take her two or three trips so no one would be suspicious.

She finally brought them all back home, what little money there was—not much, Carlos said, only about $30,000.

Growing Up Lovell

Being a child of Virgil Lovell had to have advantages.

"We were just as normal as any other kids." However, to hear Judy tell it, it was an adventure of mammoth proportions. Nevermind the normal childhood shenanigans, it was the trips to Watts Mill, the jaunts to the field trials and fox runs and the shadowing of her father, whom Judy swore hoisted the sun and deposited it in the sky, that kept life interesting.

She spent most days at Providence School—that is "until April 4 on the year I turned sixteen," when she quit in the tenth grade. She never remembered spending the night at a friend's house or even bringing a friend home. "We knowed we couldn't."

As for the necessities in life, they never did without. Virgil saw to it.

Come the first frost of the year, Virgil and Lillie would load all the children in the back of the truck and take them to Gold's Department Store in Cornelia to buy winter clothes—two each of pants, shirts, underwear and socks and one winter coat. "We'd sit on that bench, and we didn't get up like young'uns do now and go over the store," remembers Dub. "We sat there. They'd get everybody's clothes and put yours there and put your shoes there. If they didn't have one to fit, if it was a little bit big, the shoes a little big, they'd give 'em to you anyway. When they got everybody's clothes, we'd take 'em to the counter and count 'em out and that was it." There was no exchange of money; all purchases were paid for before the family walked through the doors.

"They might not be the fanciest stuff," remembers Judy, but the new clothes kept them warm in the winter and outfitted for school; even when the boys quit school, the trips to Gold's did not stop. In addition to the store-bought clothes, there were the homemade collared shirts Lillie made for the boys. There were no patterns, and they had "those hard to make collars," which drove Fred crazy when they were the slightest uneven. There were school clothes; there were play and work clothes. They were never interchanged.

The children never knew a clear reason why some were given names and others initials. Other than V.C., whose initials supposedly came from a fertilizer truck, the other initials remained a mystery. "Most of us couldn't read or write," laughs Dub, "so it was the easiest way to write our names."

Dub quit school in the eighth grade because he was needed at home on the farm. By his late teens, he had joined the army. "I had the worst time in the army. You move from one base to another," he says, and "they ask you every morning for your name, rank and serial number.

On the Lovell farm, Fred (behind the goat) and friends. *Lovell family collection.*

"'W.L. Lovell,' I'd shout.

"'I want your name!'

"'That is my name!' I'd shout back.

"'They ain't no damn body in the army with a name like that,' that officer would scream.

"'Send me home,' I tell him, 'I'm sick of this place anyhow.'"

After two years of service, he got his wish and returned home.

Discipline in the Lovell home was never questioned or ignored.

Dub and R.L. got off the school bus with instructions to head to the field to begin plowing. "We got to arguing about who was going to drive the horse," says Dub, "and daddy come over the hill with a stick. By the time he was finished with us, you could have turned that horse loose, and we'd pull the plow ourselves. We did it in a hurry. About one a year was all I needed."

Their next adventure took Dub and R.L. down to Mr. Wilbanks's cornfield. Judy tagged along, but according to her, she told them "not to do it. I was just a little thing." Since Wilbanks had planted his crop earlier in the season, the stalks were tall as Georgia pines, maturing faster, and the boys surely wouldn't let "stingy Mr. Wilbanks have it before daddy."

Dub confesses, "We went down there and pulled some of his stalks and corn and put them in our rows. He come down here and counted every

Virgil and Lillie, with Judy (kneeling), Ann and Earl. *Lovell family collection.*

stalk we got, every bushel of corn, and daddy paid him for that. After daddy finished with us, we didn't pull no more corn."

Afterward, says Judy, "he told me he was sorry he whooped me."

Families can be defined by their response to tragedy. When Dub's young wife, Thelma, died in childbirth in 1948, life changed. Without hesitation, Virgil and Lillie took Dub and Thelma's daughter, Ann, home.

"The only mother I ever knew was my grandmother," says Ann Vandiver. "I called her mama, and she was my best friend." Although there was one more at the Lovell home, Ann never did without. "I remember one Christmas when the year had been bad" and no one expected anything. "I remember I got little white ear muffs and fruit."

Dub remarried two years later and decided he wanted to bring Ann home. Judy remembers Virgil and Lillie taking her to Dub's house, and Dub asking her to go pick out her room. She remembered looking around the room and silently questioning why she was there. She knew her "room was at granddaddy's house," and there was nothing more to say.

THE LIQUOR MAKER'S DAUGHTER

It was just after midnight in November 1961. Most twelve-year-old girls were sleeping, weighed down by warming quilts during late fall cold snaps. Carlene never perfected the art of sleeping soundly. The expected notes of mountain creatures like katydids and toad frogs never lulled her into sleep; her nighttime melodies included rustling bushes and squeaky truck clutches.

Two shifts worked the shack closest to her house; the first shift kept the run moving along during the daylight hours, and the second would take over during the early morning hours. Shortly after midnight, those on the second shift would make their way past Carlos's house, signaling everything was running smoothly and that they would be taking the reins shortly. The clutch told the message.

Most nights, she lay in bed, awaiting the signal from each shift foreman. "I'd hear him put the clutch in," she says mindfully as the noise replays in her mind. "It was his signal to daddy that he was going into the shack." She knew the sound of Lloyd Free's truck as he would leave and Sherrill Smith's truck as he would arrive to relieve him of his shift. She would pull the covers up underneath her chin snuggly, knowing the shifts had changed and signals were received. Her daddy was safe, and she could sleep.

On this night, instead of the sound of clutches, police lights sliced the darkness, lighting up the night sky heading north toward her uncle's house. Since her bed would not bring comfort this night, she sat on the hope chest beneath the window, her knees drawn up. By morning, nearly 1,200 gallons of liquor had been confiscated, and her uncle and her daddy were arrested and shut down. It was the end of clutch sounds—for a while.

This reality was Carlene's perpetual fear. "I didn't talk about it. I was very conscious of it. I knew what was going on; I wasn't dumb. I simply kept my head in a book."

Even today, she doesn't sleep well. She calls it being wired. In her mind, she didn't "think he cared or realized" how it affected her, and the ship he ran, as she describes it, was tough. She lived in constant fear of "daddy getting caught."

Much like other children of liquor makers, she rarely had friends come to her house. "I could only have three girls, and it had to be someone whose daddy that daddy trusted because if they were to see something," they would go home and tell their parent, raising all kinds of questions. "I would always panic if I got assigned a project [at school] and it was with someone else because I knew it wasn't going to work."

Growing up was tough, she continues. Her entire life was a rule. With three knocks of the pocketknife on her bedroom door, she knew it meant to get up and "you better not be long about it." There were schedules to be maintained. There was cattle to show, and since her brother, Virgil, wasn't old enough, Carlene was "the next best thing. He made me work with them every day and practice. He told me if 'you ever turn that steer loose, you'll be sorry you did.'" To this day, she holds tightly.

"I minded my own business," she says. Her father didn't come home and tell stories about how many gallons he produced or how many revenuers were slinking around the woods. Back then, children did not talk about what was not their business. "I knew I wasn't allowed to ask questions. My mindset growing up with daddy was this: you didn't talk about it, and it was my job to do whatever I needed to do in school."

Carlene tagged along with her father "whenever she could." He would tell her to stay in the truck as he walked away to look at cows. "I always minded him, and when he would come back, I would be in the floorboard, all curled up on the ropes."

Richard Drake in *Appalachia* notes that "the coming of schools brought a broadening of opportunities and a wider awareness of the world." In the early years, children in the northern part of the county attended Providence School until the mid-'60s, when children were transported into Clarkesville for their education. Since Carlene's home address was Clarkesville, she attended school there. As the boundaries and opportunities expanded, so did the complexities.

And in that setting, problems arose. With her mother teaching school and her father working the farm, both were very busy. Carlene had to take care

Carlos and Carlene, circa late 1970s. *Carlene Holder.*

of things, for "if something happened at school and he found out, I'd be in worse trouble."

"I didn't want to bother them because I never knew where anybody was," tells Carlene. "There was this man named Mr. Jenkins. He was the taxi driver. Daddy would pay him, and he would take me home. One day, I stayed after school. I was at a GA [Girls Auxiliary] meeting. Somehow I couldn't get ahold of Mr. Jenkins. The school office was closed. I don't remember how I got in touch with Daddy. He came up. I can just see him. I must have been in the sixth or seventh grade. I always took home every one of my books. He pulled in, and he was mad. He said, 'Get in. I'm running late.'" As Carlos drove home, Carlene remembers them being pulled over alongside the highway by a group of men and being told that the law was "up the road," waiting for him.

And in high school, arranging for pickup was the easy issue.

"They would call me the liquor maker's daughter," says Carlene. Inside the classroom or down the hall, it did not matter. "I was in the tenth or eleventh grade, and Ernest Hightower was standing there and heard them call me that. I was in chemistry, sitting on stools, and John Bishop came in and said, 'Well, I wanna tell you, I hauled hay yesterday for the liquor maker's daughter's dad.'"

Like most farmers in the area, the Lovells hired young boys for baling hay and doing chores around the farm. Most knew of the rumored stills, but most kept their mouth shut and eyes closed to things that were none of their concern. "You don't mess with the Lovells," for they had a reputation.

Carlene looked at Ernest Hightower with begging eyes, pleading for his help, but he did not come to her aid. "He didn't say a word. About that time, very unexpectedly, Hollace Harrison and Johnny Crosby came over and picked John up. One took one arm and one took the other." All three disappeared into the hallway. "You could hear lockers outside being hit. John came back in and since that day, never said another word."

It was in church where Carlene received her most eye-opening education.

"I went to church with Grandma Wilbanks [maternal grandmother]," says Carlene. "They went to church all the time. I loved going to church. We'd go to Clarkesville Baptist Church, and the ladies there were so nice to me. I was in Girls Auxiliary, but then one time, the preacher's daughter said, 'I think we should put Carlene on the prayer list.' I wondered why. She said, 'Because of the liquor and what a terrible life you have.' I was furious. They were in church."

Being sheltered within a small southern town, Carlene longed to learn of the world beyond Clarkesville. "I always wanted to go somewhere," says Carlene. "I always wanted to see. I don't know how old I was, but Judy asked me to go with her to a dog show in Alabama; I just jumped at it. I just wanted to go." On rare occasions, it was mainly she and her mother who traveled beyond Clarkesville. Going to the World's Fair in New York in 1964 was a delight; keeping a journal along the way, Carlene logged every bridge crossing and every open field from Clarkesville to New York City.

When it got time to move on, she did. Although she wanted to go, she wanted to stay more, choosing the nearby University of Georgia in Athens, Georgia, for college and Brenau in Gainesville, Georgia, for teaching. Following in her mother's footsteps and later heeding her mother's advice of not allowing the job to consume her, she left teaching. It could not have been scripted any better that she met Jack Holder at a cattle sale in Durham, North Carolina. They dated for two years, then married and made Charlotte, North Carolina, their home. Her son, Lovell—her "magnus opus," as she calls him—was born in 1986.

"Growing up around whiskey," says Carlene, "I can honestly tell you, I never had a drop of liquor after I went to school, all through college. Never had any, period. I was a Miss Goody-Two-Shoes. I'm making up for it now."

LEARNING THE SIGNS

Martha Bristol, the daughter of V.L. Lovell, believes it was easier living in Batesville as opposed to surrounding communities because there were so many people involved in illegal liquor production. "If anyone was picking on kids from other families, we'd tell them, 'hush,' and they didn't know what they was talking about. You don't know nothing about my daddy."

Similar to her cousins' experiences, no classmates came home with her. "It was OK if they were from Batesville because it [was] hard to find someone who didn't work in the still, run the still or help sell what the still made."

Providence School in Batesville closed, and Martha became a rookie in the eighth grade at North Habersham High School in Clarkesville.

I was the only one from Providence in that grade, and if [it] hadn't been for Betty Jean Congdon and Catherine Logan, I don't know what I would have done. Mrs. Congdon just took me in. I'll never forget there was this guy who always called me the liquor still girl. One day, I had just had it. I held up my hand and asked Mrs. Congdon, "Is it all right if I slap Bobby?" She said, "Please do." I hauled back and gave him a ringer and said, "Don't you ever say that again." You always had a place in your heart for anyone who took up for you.

Most agreed that they were just kids in school, trying to bring attention to themselves, but the gravity of their words bore deep holes.

It was 1961 before she was allowed to date; she was sixteen. By that time, she had graduated from high school and was on her way to Berry College. She was able to make her own decisions about whom to date and whom to befriend.

And in regards to seeing the still, none of the children were ever allowed to go deep into the woods, except one time when Martha and her brother Ronnie were the lucky ones.

"There was a man [who] worked for daddy," she remembers. "Something happened to one of his family members. There wasn't anyone at home [who] could go get him, so me and Ronnie [her brother] had to go down to the woods to tell him he had to come out of the woods. He was over at Brock Branch holler. When we got there, the still was running and they said, 'You get outta here! Your daddy will have a fit.' We gave him the message and came straight back." That was the only time Martha ever saw a still until her visit to Ivy Mountain Distillery in Mount Airy.

For those who didn't grow up in Batesville, they understood little of what happened at home, although they thought they did.

Martha feels sure the others "pictured our homes like this: if our parents made it [liquor], they drank to excess.

"Daddy always had all kinds of legal liquor in a cabinet," Martha continues. "If some of his friends came, and he would want to offer them a drink, he had it."

"He would say to us, 'If you want to know what liquor tastes like, it's in the cabinet. You taste it. See what happens when you drink, and how you act when you've had too much drink. Don't you wait till you get out in public and try it 'cause you'll be embarrassed.'" Martha never took her father up on that offer primarily because she saw how it changed people.

The only change she took part in was the healing kind. "Moonshine was our medicine," says Martha. "We would have like peppermint, honey and whiskey for coughs and colds and when you were having your monthly. Grandma would take whiskey and put cinnamon and peppermint and something else in it. She would burn it to get the alcohol out and you'd drink it right down. You could trace it all the way to your stomach."

There were signs everywhere, and a moonshiner, as well as his children, had to be well versed in reading each one.

"I remember what kind of car every revenue officer owned," remembers Martha. "We knew them by sight. We knew not to say anything to them. We would be riding our bicycles on the side of the road, and they knew us. They'd stop and say, 'Where's your daddy today? Is he at the liquor still?' I was always the assigned spokesperson 'cause I could look really indignant at them. I'd say, 'You ought to be ashamed of yourself. My daddy don't have no liquor still.'"

If the revenuers ventured into their front yard with questions, the answer was always the same: "In the field."

Then there were always the usual people in the community who made a habit out of turning alleged moonshiners over to the law. Martha knew of a "couple of churchgoing ladies [who] if they ever found out you were running a still, they would call and report you, and according to most, if you were reported, the law had to check." Every community had those people whose attention was everywhere except where it needed to be. Martha recalls one check-in:

> Daddy knew that he had been reported, and he had to move everything he possibly could. But they [the law] had to do something about it. They had

fingerprints on somebody. So, David Ayers and Bub Kay [federal agents] headed to our house. David Ayers had a knife that had a blade on it that was real shiny. He was holding it by the handle, and he was whittling something. He said, "V.L., have you ever seen a knife like this" and hands it to daddy. Daddy says, "Lord, my hands are dirty," and he reaches back and gets a handkerchief and brings it out and takes it with the handkerchief. He looks it over real good, and says, "I've never seen one like this" and hands it back and never touches it. I'll never forget as a kid looking at David Ayers's face like, "Damn, I didn't get it."

There were the moonshine moments, but the most important were those times spent with grandparents.

After Martha helped her grandmother in the house with the cooking and dishes, she said she "could go with granddaddy. He taught me all those things that every refined southern lady ought to know. How to dig worms, how to bait a hook, how to cast out and catch a bass, whether it was a good place to catch one or not, how to trout fish." Once the craft of fishing was learned, she was on to horses. "I would have to clean out the hoofs, brush the horse down. He'd make me clean the saddle when I got through riding. I had to take care of all that stuff. He would watch me and say, 'You're not holding your feet right' or, 'You need to sit up a little straighter.'"

The last time they saddled up together was shortly before she left for college. "He had bought a horse for Judy that had a white blaze on its face. I was riding it up a hill and a little ol' cat scooted from one tree to another and the horse reared up. I sat on him and calmed it down."

"Get off him right now," he pleaded. She rode him back to the barn, and when she returned the next day, the horse was gone.

"I don't want her hurt," her grandfather said in explaining his decision. Knowing she was upset, he promised her a new horse when she came home from college.

It wasn't the fishing or the horses, explains Martha. "It was spending time with him. I will always believe he hung the moon."

A CHAMPION'S TAKE: A NARRATIVE

"That's the picture that mama gave daddy years ago." Judy points to a small framed painting, one of six, all differing in size, hanging over her living room

Judy positions her dog at a bench trial. *Lovell family collection.*

sofa in her home just off Highway 441 in Clarkesville. "She bought that in Clayton. Paid seventy-nine cents for it. Of course, I had it framed."

The picture was of men mounted on horses surrounded by black-and-tan foxhounds, bouncing wildly and eager for the chase. Every photograph told the same tale of men, their horses and their dogs.

It was a man's world in the 1950s, and Judy found herself right in the middle, competing against men who were stunned at the thought of her being there. When most women would shrink from such opportunities, Judy accepted them as a challenge, ones she would surely win.

"I'd beat their butt and go on. I didn't care how they felt about me. I didn't stick around to find out."

Generally, she was the only girl showing dogs; plus, she had to take the challenge in a dress, which proved difficult. "I's about the only woman showing other than one judge's wife [who] showed. The boys said I done it 'cause I was the only girl. I'd tell them, 'Shut your mouth. I done it 'cause I had the best dog.'"

Her father's reputation was clear, and it did not take her long to develop one as well. Once Carlos stopped showing, it was Judy and her daddy who traveled from Florida to Tennessee in search of silver.

"Me and daddy would go to the field trial," tells Judy. This particular one was in South Carolina. "We'd have the truck loaded down with dogs. I'd jump out, get my dogs out. We'd have to tie them to the tree with chains. It's not like it is now. We'd put 'em out and take care of 'em."

Competitors turned into scouts as the Lovells would unload their pack of dogs.

"We'd start putting numbers on dogs and turning them loose, and everybody was looking at what we had. This ol' boy come up."

Quietly and respectfully, he said, "Mr. Lovell, your dogs is too big to run in this territory. You can't do nothing here. You might as well go back home."

Virgil wasn't much for words. "He wasn't like his kids," Judy quips.

"Son," Virgil replies, "Mine'll make a trail for yours to go through."

The three of them took their place in the boy's truck and rode the unknown territory.

"I seen ol' Lemon coming across the field," says Judy. "Everything was behind him. That boy's eyes looked like saucers."

"How did that dog get through that thicket," he asks. "He's in front of everybody."

"Daddy never once said 'I told you so' to that boy, but we knew the dog had just won the show."

In a manner of speaking, Carlos taught Judy how to show dogs. "I watched Carlos, and he beat me enough till I learned how to beat him. I wanted to win, and I couldn't win unless I beat him. He was always on the front bench."

The legacy of Judy's artful command of hounds lives within the stacked silver platters, bowls and coffee pots etched with the dates and names of front bench victories. Photographs are everywhere, and she explains how she "just knows" how to handle the dog. Her face beams and her voice drops as she focuses the dog's attention. "Hold it. Hold it for mama," she says. The dog freezes, tail trumpeted, waiting for his release. "Good boy," she says.

Her last win in 2012 with Banker (What's in Your Pocket) at Granada, Mississippi, put her back on the front bench with a National Championship.

V

LUCKY AT THE SHACK AND ON THE ROAD

Liquor in barrels is better than money in the bank.
—Virge Lovell

Outside the mountains, they were called moonshiners; inside the mountains, they were called blockaders, according to museum curator Barry Stiles of the Foxfire Museum in Clayton, Georgia. Situated on the rugged side of Black Rock Mountain, the museum and heritage center exhibit authentic structures dating back some 180 years and present artifacts that have no rhyme or reason for younger generations. From the chapel with the split-log pews to the gristmill with half-ton millstones, it represents a bygone era that few recall. Just beyond the chapel, on a bluff shrouded in leaves and brush is a moonshine still, crafted by Rabun County's premier liquor maker, Buck Carver.

"It is a replica of what he would have used," explains Stiles as he rakes back leaves and moss that conceal it from prying eyes. "He chose the location, just like what he would have done [for an illegal still]." It is a small still that would produce a typical runoff of twelve gallons, and although working ones would have "a little more design involved," it is hardly noticeable—perfection by moonshiner standards.

A blockader all his life, Carver began making liquor at the age of eighteen and sold it from his house deep within the hollers of the Chattahoochee Forest of Rabun County. He stopped when his "health got so bad I couldn't make it and the law got so bad the means didn't justify the risk," he told the *L.A. Herald Examiner* in 1973.

People in the mountains just weren't interested in changing, says Stiles of their daily way of living or their moonshining ways. "It's mystical with a lot of romance associated with it."

Many still pine for that way of life, where mountains envelop and simplicity prevails and a man can simply do as he wants. Its lament shaped a melody created in 1967 when songwriters Boudleaux Bryant and Felice Bryant locked themselves away in room 388 at the Gatlinburg Inn in the mountain hamlet of Gatlinburg, Tennessee, and created a jewel that provided a voice for all mountain folk. It took as little as ten minutes to link the words together that expressed a universal sentiment regarding their way of life and their noble profession:

> *Once two strangers climbed on rocky top,*
> *Lookin' for a moonshine still.*
> *Strangers ain't come back from rocky top,*
> *Guess they never will.*
> *Corn won't grow at all on rocky top,*
> *Dirt's too rocky by far.*
> *That's why all the folks on rocky top*
> *Get their corn from a jar.*
> *Rocky top, you'll always be*
> *Home sweet home to me.*
> *Good ole rocky top,*
> *Rocky top Tennessee, rocky top Tennessee.*

No matter which piece of the Appalachian Mountains held your rocky top, everyone echoed this mystical bias of their beloved spot on earth. How you choose to label mountain life and this questionable profession—moonshining or blockading or running—remains a detailed lens through which you can gain insight into the culture and motivations of the Appalachian people.

MOONSHINE POCKETS

In *Moonshine Spirits*, Joseph Dabney labels certain areas as "moonshine pockets," hollers and corners within the rural South where the scope of moonshine production was enough to make your head spin. Not everyone could see it, but everyone knew it was there. All locales had

Revenuers bust a still in North Carolina. *Richard Miller.*

commonalities—"a longtime liquor-making tradition; a lack of economic opportunity, and a location relatively near metropolitan centers where the booze could be marketed easily and profitably." Furthermore, Peine and Schafft believe "scores of people considered respectable and law-abiding by their community were suddenly deemed criminals by the apparatus of the state." Federals scoured these moonshine pockets and their liable producers, all in the name of giving the government its due.

According to Dabney, there were four counties named as "moonshine capitals of America: Dawson County, Georgia; Cocke County, Tennessee; Franklin County, Virginia; and Wilkes County, North Carolina."

Georgia's primary pocket was Dawsonville in northwest Dawson County. According to Dabney, "There was hardly a mile along any stream in the area that was not at one time 'decorated' with a copper pot," and by the early 1940s, Dawson and its surrounding counties were "pumping upward of a million gallons of whiskey a year into Atlanta." Production was hefty, and with it came an entirely new challenge: how to get orders to their customers. Handling the backwoods dirt roads with speed proved difficult until one day in the early 1930s. Bootleggers discovered the magic of added carburetors and sturdy shock absorbers and left the law in the dust. Known as "trippers," they navigated in and out of sharp turns as they left a streak from Dawsonville to Atlanta.

Because of these souped-up cars with enigmatic drivers behind the wheel, legends were born. "Bootleggers became folk heroes as they stealthily drove cars of whiskey out from the mountain hollows and down into the thirsty cities of Atlanta, Asheville, Memphis, Greenville, Knoxville, and Charlotte," describes Neal Thompson in *Driving with the Devil*.

Smoke billowed from the mountaintops of Cocke County, Tennessee, a town held prisoner by rugged terrain. One bootlegger told writers Peine and Schafft in *Moonshine, Mountaineers and Modernity* that he worked "ten hours a day and you can't make a living. You can live, but you can't make a good living. You gotta do something else." Moonshine emerged from economic necessity and survival. They quote one moonshiner as claiming, "You had the people that made the stills, you had the people that fixed the cars, and all these different things…[there] was a garage for years where they outfitted cars with those suspension systems…that the cars [people] brought [in to be modified for running liquor were what kept the business alive]."

Some escaped the wrath of the law while other enterprising folk with good intentions and bad luck spent time in prison. The old-timers viewed the possibility of capture as an "occupational hazard" and saw the ability to evade the federal and local powers as a source of pride. The area's most legendary entrepreneur, Marvin "Popcorn" Sutton, learned to distill in these woods and, according to Duay O'Neil and the *New York Times*, "gave the world what they expected of a moonshiner. He dressed the part and he talked the talk." Contemplating the legalization of his home elixir and before his death in 2009, Sutton discussed with county officials the possibility of opening a distillery and museum in Cocke County, with officials understanding his legacy as "a potentially rich source of tax revenue in a county that has its economic struggles." Even before 2012, when it became legal for distilleries to operate in Parrottsville, whiskey distillers knew Sutton's cult value, and government officials had no choice but to listen—that is, if they wanted to reap the rewards. And today, tourists flock here "to see and experience what they have been led to believe is a disappearing way of life."

Farther north, another "moonshine capital of the world" was Franklin County, Virginia. In 1935, federal officials estimated that the government had been duped out of $5.5 million in taxes (based on the 1920 tax rate). Known as the Conspiracy Trial of 1935, the two-month trial ended a seven-year run for local officials, according to the *Franklin News Post*, who had "moved more than a million gallons of whiskey out of the county during the period covered in the indictment, traveling in caravans at high speed with 'pilot' cars running interference to 'ward off any officers that tried to stop them.'" The newspaper reported that a "total of 37 tons of yeast, 16,920 tons of sugar and thousands of tons of malt, meal and other materials" had gone through Franklin County.

For the farmer in Franklin County, says Burkhard Bilger in *Moonshine, Monster Catfish and Other Southern Comforts*, it was the ideal instrument for " concentrating profits." Heavy production continued throughout the later part of the century, and by 2000, it was estimated that moonshiners produced "close to a million gallons a year" throughout the Appalachians with "the lion's share of it in Franklin County."

Although Habersham County was no Dawson or Franklin County, the area provided a steady stream of illegal spirits transported into major cities. Lovell liquor traveled as far away as New York. Fred averaged four loads a week out of his Batesville shack, a working shack for over five years, to locations like Jefferson and Athens but only as far south as Griffin. Most of the time, it followed the main road from Habersham County to the Atlanta Farmers' Market where, in addition to illegal liquor, government liquor [legal] was sold. Vendors would put legal liquor in barrels, claims Fred, and sell it over the counter. Once a request was made for the illegal kind, the seller emptied the bottled government liquor and refilled it with Lovell liquor. The Lovells charged sixteen to eighteen dollars a case (six gallons), and cases were in high demand; government liquor was twice the price and, usually, half the proof.

MEANWHILE IN NORTH CAROLINA

Moonshining in the Appalachians rode the tailwind post-Prohibition demand for cheap liquor. For distillers across the North Carolina line, it was Carolina moonshine that moved the trucks and proved that Wilkes County was, indeed, on fire.

Whiskey had been crafted in Wilkes County since the mid-1700s and continued to be until 1935, when Wilkes County held claim to the largest seizure of illegal liquor in American history. That significant bust did little to deter illegal producers.

Even at eighty-three, Junior Johnson remembers it like it was yesterday.

"The house was plum full of whiskey. We had to crawl across the whiskey to get in the bed." Just four years old, Junior saw it as a magical maze, not a covert warehouse filled with cardboard cases of illegal gallon jugs.

It was an unspoken rule among moonshiners that evidence remained as far away from home as possible, and it was pure luck when the revenuers descended on the Glenn Johnson home in 1935. Informants disclosed the possibility of a still on his property, unusually close to his house, and that was what they sought. Instead, they landed the mother lode.

Revenuers in black gangster-style suits and Fedoras descended on Ingle Hollow, shocking the Johnson family.

"The officers nailed some boards so that they could slide it [cases of liquor] down the steps [from the upstairs] instead of carrying it. Well, me and my brother Fred, we'd jump on them cases and ride them down and then go back up. They'd say, 'You young'uns get outta here.' We'd tell them, 'You get outta here. This is our home.' We'd run back and forth and ride 'em back down again till they got all the whiskey out of the upstairs. You wouldn't believe that it was in the house."

Junior remembers his father peering from the sidelines.

"He just stood there and watched it a little while thinking about what he was going to do. They didn't arrest him. They knew he was going to jail. They was busting it up, and he was standing there watching it. They kept on doing it. He kinda eased off to the side a little bit and then disappeared. He stayed at a friend's house for about two months before he turned himself in."

It was a chaotic time in the distilling business, and "the revenuers got hot on everybody [who] was hauling and making whiskey. They got kinda cut down, and they wouldn't move as much in Winston-Salem and places like that. The revenuers was arresting everybody, and they slowed up, and he [daddy] kept making it, and it just got backed up."

A record 7,100 gallons of corn whiskey was confiscated, amounting to over $28,000 in taxes and penalties due the federal government. As had become tradition after the prideful apprehension, maybe as a cautionary tale to those who contemplated starting all over again the next morning, the revenuers took their ceremonial photograph with the payoff before glass and white lightning showered the lawn.

It wasn't the first time for Glenn Johnson, and it wouldn't be his last. "He got caught five times. They got to where they knew him in the penitentiary. He'd get caught and get two years. In about three or four months, they'd turn him loose, and he'd go back home." And he went back to the still every time.

Lora Belle Money and Robert Glenn Johnson taught their seven children that even though times were tough, push on through.

"My dad was probably the biggest and the best," says Johnson, who said if he could grow up and be like his father, he would be happy and satisfied with his life. And of course, "he always had the name of having the best moonshine."

Revenuers seize 7,100 gallons of corn whiskey in 1935 in Wilkes County, North Carolina, at the home of Glenn Johnson. *Junior Johnson.*

"He growed the corn, and they would feed the cows corn from the farm. My mother would can corn. When we got enough corn canned and enough to feed the cows through the winters, he'd always make sure he had enough and when he had too much, he'd make whiskey."

Junior looks back at his grandfather Roscoe Johnson making whiskey and describes him as a "pretty aggressive person." Both his grandfather and his father were self-taught and very smart, and Junior attributes his somewhat questionable behavior at times as a legacy to their teachings of endurance.

"It was a tough life back in them days." Junior remembers that helping meant taking family in or "putting five or six young'uns in the same bed." But when his father got into the liquor business, some fifteen years before it took off, he was the only one "who had lights in his house. He was smart and determined to do what wasn't supposed to be done."

It was Junior and the two elder brothers—Fred and L.P.—who helped their father, but it was their father who crafted the spirits. At the beginning, they would simply help "at the building down below the barn" that had the little moonshine still. "I didn't know what he was doing. I was just helping him. I soon learned how to do it, and as I come on up, I more or less perfected it to suit what I needed."

Of his teacher, Junior says he "was a different kind of individual. He used [a] fifty-gallon metal drum to do the heating with it and made his stills

Junior Johnson. *Junior Johnson.*

out of wood, but he did use a copper radiator out of a car to cool it and bring it from steam to whiskey. Later on, he did copper, he'd run it up the creek, down the creek, and he'd just use the copper pipe to cool it."

At fourteen, Junior started hauling for his daddy, and by age twenty, he was on his own.

"When I married and moved out and went out on my own in the bootlegging business, I hauled it for years. Got to where I needed fast cars, and I got to working on them and making them faster and faster."

For ten years, whenever people needed a guaranteed delivery, it was Junior's name that was synonymous with transport. Reportedly making anywhere from "$350 to $450 a night hauling whiskey to cities and mill towns in the Piedmont," Junior hustled. Locations and methods, well, Junior can rattle them off like the names of good friends.

"Ellijay, Dawsonville, I knowed them like the back of my hand, even Gulf Port and Biloxi. I had tractor-trailers hauling out of Biloxi, Mississippi. Ships would come in, and before [they] got [to] the ABC store, they would take it off the ships and sell it to you because they didn't want no record. You'd just back in there. The red liquor wasn't in every state. There wasn't a law against it [red liquor] here [Mississippi], but when you got back home, there was a law against it."

Daniel Pierce confirms in *Real NASCAR* that "another aspect of the illegal alcohol business" was transporting red liquor or "federal tax–paid whiskey bottled by legal distillers." Much of the South remained dry after Prohibition, and demand for red liquor rose. Of this, Pierce states that "moonshiners—already on the wrong side of the law—stepped in to meet that need, hauling the stuff in by the tractor-trailer load in many cases." Junior Johnson trafficked both, illegal moonshine and red liquor.

"My biggest customers I had [were in] Indianapolis. Believe it or not, Indianapolis had the mafia in it. I hauled sugar back for the bootleggers, whiskey to Dawsonville and go on from there. I'd pick up sugar and bring it back to Wilkes County people."

If people weren't calling him for deliveries, he knew how to get in touch with them.

I knew how to get the customers. Just like over here, coming up here in Salisbury. I knew five people in Salisbury, and they handled the whole area plum down to Altamont with white liquor. He done deliver their liquor to them every night in some storage place. It was almost like a taxi-cab, set it up to where you met your time frame on time. You didn't have any trouble.

I did [run] through a guy in the mafia in Indianapolis and Philadelphia. I'd go to Biloxi and pick up a load of white liquor. There was two guys down there and [I'd] call them this morning and be down there tomorrow night and pick up 575 cases—six gallons in a case—in a tractor-trailer and pull it back to Philadelphia. The guy would meet me at the end of the Virginia Turnpike, and he'd follow that truck everywhere it went until it went to a certain truck stop. He would watch that truck. You'd get out of it, 'cause I had a car that followed that truck. I didn't want to leave a driver somewhere. He'd get in the car with the guy that got out of the truck and left the keys in it. We'd go to a restaurant and about an hour; we'd come back, and the truck would be sitting back there. And it would be empty.

Aw, it was easy, if you were working with people you trust. At one time, I was working with about five hundred people.

And if you missed a drop-off or had problems?

If you miss that time and the person leaves, you're hung out. You had to bring the whiskey back, but I always had places to drop it off.

I had a bunch of my friends working with me. I didn't work [with] anybody I didn't trust. It was really kind of funny. I had two white drivers on each one of my tractor-trailers. Back in them days, you had to go through a weigh station, and they'd ask what you had on. We had them little boxes on the back door full of corn, and we'd say, "Corn." They'd go to the back and pick them boxes up and see the corn. They couldn't open the doors, 'cause the corn would fall out on the ground. Had a little ole motor sitting up front running cool into them [trailers].

It was 575 cases packed solid in a tractor-trailer; in a car, 22 was magic.

"Two in the floorboard in front, two across the door, sit one beside you and the rest of it in the back. Twenty-two cases made a solid level playing field, below the windows and no one could see."

And it was in these cars with two superchargers that the bootleg turn was born:

> *I had the advantage on them. I had a big motor and a fast car. They just had a regular car, and they couldn't catch you unless your car tore up. They would try to block the roads and stuff. Even when they got after you, the first thing you'd do is get a little run on 'em, and turn around and meet 'em. You right quick get on the brakes and get down as slow as you can. Pull off on the side of the road and spin that thing around. Sometimes they didn't even know it was you.*

At the age of twenty-three, Junior left moonshining for racing.

A year later, in 1956, he led for 150 laps in the only race he would ever compete in at Altamont, New York, and brought home a purse of $900.

> *I drove all night to get back home. Come in about 4:30 in the morning at the house. My daddy had a still back over in the woods. You have to fire a still up before daylight because it smokes when you first build a fire. People will see it and report you. He had overslept and asked me to go fire the still up. So I went and fired up the still, and I was waiting on him. He had the horse and wagon and the stuff you needed to put the whiskey in, and put his beer back to work. The revenuers had found his still, and he didn't know. There's eighteen revenuers around it, and I was in the middle of 'em.*
>
> *They's all hid. I heard my dad coming in the wagon, and I had the fire going. It had done quit smoking, and it was running real good. There's a coal—coke—that you can burn that don't smoke. I decided I'd shovel some it in the fire so he wouldn't have to do it, and it was going real good. I had some of it poured out in a box where I could shovel it, and [when] I reached down to shovel the coal and I heard something.*
>
> *I still had the shovel in my hand. I turned around and there was an officer coming straight at me, gonna jump on my back. I gave him that shovel and coke, and I took off running. He starting hollering to all those officers, "Catch Junior Johnson cause he's coming down through there." I thought he was just bluffing, and I kept running. I knew there was a gap in*

the fence, and I knowed I could out-run a deer when I was little. I missed that gap and got tangled up in that fence, and they caught me.

Having caught the uncatchable, the justice system sentenced Junior to two years in the penitentiary in Chillicothe, Ohio.

Junior told *Esquire* writer Tom Wolf, who dubbed Junior the Last American Hero in 1965:

That was one good thing about Chillicothe. I don't want to pull any more time, but I wouldn't take anything in the world for the experience I had in prison. If a man needed to change, that was the place to change. H'it's not a waste of time there, h'it's good experience. H'it's that they's so many people in the world that feel that nobody is going to tell them what to do. I had quite a temper, I reckon. I always had the idea that I had as much sense as the other person and I didn't want them to tell me what to do. In the penitentiary there I found out that I could listen to another fellow and be told what to do and h'it wouldn't kill me.

He served eleven months, three days.

Even with a stretch in the federal penitentiary, Junior "moonlighted in the family business in 1958" according to *Real Nascar.* His financial obligation to his family surpassed common sense. Author Daniel Pierce quotes Junior as saying, "I could have walked away real quick like, but what would that have meant for my family? When I made money from moonshine, it was their money too. How could I just cut off the money?" In September 1958, federal agents cleaned up Wilkes County, breaking up sixteen stills, one on the Johnson property. The Johnson home was raided, and Junior; his brothers; and his mother, Lora Belle, were arrested. Both brothers were found guilty and, in addition to a fine, given prison time; his mother received an eight-month suspended sentence and a $7,500 fine. Junior was found not guilty of all charges.

Then, Junior "got to going real good in racing and never looked back again." He returned to NASCAR and, over the next two years, won eleven races. Then in 1960, with a car that was twenty-two-miles-per-hour slower than the top cars, he uncovered the slipstream of the car ahead and, accommodated with "drafting," won at Daytona in 1960 at the age of twenty-nine, the youngest ever. With his $25,000 cut of the purse, he invested in one chicken house, which began his long lucrative relationship with Holly Farms as a chicken producer and stock car driver.

Junior Johnson during early NASCAR days.
Junior Johnson.

He retired in 1966 with fifty race victories, attributing much of his success to bootlegging. "Moonshiners put more time, energy, thought and love into their cars than any racer ever will. Lose on the track, and you go home. Lose with a load of whiskey, and you go to jail."

One could say that moonshine forged Junior's future. Today, his legitimate distillery, Midnight Moon, relies on his father's recipe as "the only recipe that you can have a life span with."

He admits that he had "no limits" financially, and "I done what I done. I've lived a great life. I don't know how I did it. I never took on anything that I didn't think I could be the best [at]. I'd leave it alone if I didn't think I could be the top person. I succeeded because I wouldn't give up. I had the mentality, or the craziness, not to give up."

As for which money was sweeter—money made winning races or money made making moonshine—he "tells the honest God's truth. Both of them was parallel. Both were just exactly alike. You stayed up all night to race. You stayed up all night long to make moonshine, and the harder you worked, the better you were at racing, and the harder you worked, the more money you made at moonshine. It was a determined thing. You could slide over from one to another and didn't miss a thing."

And finally, he calls the moonshiners the more honest of the two: "Racers are people [who] will steal from you and lie to you. A moonshiner won't do that. A good moonshiner is as honest as the day is long."

VI

ON THE WRONG SIDE
OF THE LAW

The sun don't shine on the same dog's hind end all the time.
—Virge Lovell

Moonshine production numbers heralded the 1950s and 1960s the most lucrative decades in illegal distilling in American history. Even though the 1935 record seizure of 7,100 cases at the Johnson home in Wilkes County, North Carolina, might have panicked a few enterprising distillers, for the most part, it did little to stop or slow them down. In 1951, the *Washington Post* reported that "more bootleg whisky is being made and sold today than during the prohibition era."

It was big business—bootlegger style—as deep-seated pockets overflowed with cash from normally law-abiding citizens. Around 1951, the national average tax on a gallon of liquor was $11.57. Once distillers added the state taxes and other required fees, their profit was nil. The *Post* stated, "Federal, State and local authorities seized 19,644 stills with a daily production capacity of 677,179 gallons. On a five-day week, they could have produced 176,066,540 gallons of moonshine. On a round the clock basis, which is the way most bootleggers operate their stills, they were capable of turning out 247,170,335 gallons of illegal booze or the equivalent of 1,225,851,675 fifth bottles of illegal whisky."

In 1950, it cost a licensed distiller, on average, $12.00 a gallon to distill and store his whiskey in charred oak casks for the desired four years. An average fifth sold at $3.75, with the federal and state share at $2.10, or more than half. The *Post* wrote that the bootlegger can "release his product at the still for around $3 a gallon" with an operating profit of better than 200 percent. On average, bootleg whiskey "in most cities of the country runs about $1 a pint and $2 a fifth." It was almost a certainty that after the sale of the first run, the physical still was paid for and everything else was pure profit.

American Moonshine attributes the increase to the "technological advancements in moonshine distilling" during these two decades. "The number of federally seized stills was dropping but the capacity of the seized stills was dramatically on the rise. An estimated 90 percent of the moonshine distilled in the United States was made in the South with Alabama and Georgia on top of the list. One out of every five gallons of liquor produced in the U.S. at that time was illegal moonshine."

Horace Kephart believes that it was the "intention of the Revenue Department...not to inflame the mountain people, but to treat them as considerately as possible." These men had concluded that "the fraud of illicit distilling was an evil too firmly established to be uprooted, and that it must be endured." Lightheartedly, he concluded that "a man has the same right to make his own whiskey as his own soup."

However, much like the moonshiners, the revenuers had families to feed and jobs to complete. So they rambled through every briar patch, backwoods thicket and creek bed on every mountain in North Georgia. According to historian William Raper, Highway 197 was the main road for hauling out of Rabun County as well as for distributing what was produced in Habersham County; it was a hot spot that was crawling with revenuers.

"There's been enough liquor hauled up and down 197 to float the *Queen Mary* several times, if she's dry-docked," believes Fred. "I know I made enough."

A LOVE-HATE RELATIONSHIP

Deep within the Habersham-Rabun Country territory, federal agents infiltrated the deep woods and hollers, and every moonshiner knew them by face, car and reputation. It was rumored that the federals stopped at Piedmont College on their way to Batesville, picking up a few baseball players to assist in the chase. Everyone knew that the federals revenuers couldn't run fast.

No agent was more memorable than Bub Kay. Joseph Dabney references him in *Moonshine Spirits*, commenting that most moonshiners mispronounced his name, calling him Bub McKay. I found that stumbling block as well. Of

Kay, Dabney writes that he played "fair and square," and quite simply, "he was greatly loved by all the members of the corn likker fraternity, even when he arrested them." One old-timer told Dabney that Kay was "as good an officer as I ever seed in my life. I don't believe he would swear a thing in the world on you but what he knowed." He was known for cutting a shack down and then, afterward, sitting down at the moonshiner's dinner table before hauling them off to jail.

A local-federal, as they called him, Bub Kay got out of his car and stood in Virgil Lovell's front yard. It was spring around 1950, and as far as the eyes could see, promising green pastures.

"You know," he said, slowly so there wouldn't be any doubt, "I don't mind seeing a man make liquor that don't have anything to make." He stopped and turned toward Virgil's pasture, pausing to consider everything in front of him. "Boy, look at all those Black Angus cattle in that field. Ain't they purdy? This beautiful grass and all this stuff." And then he turned, got back in a car and left in a cloud of dust.

Virgil squirmed until Kay's customary 1939 Ford left his sight before he hollered down the hill at Fred. "Get across that hill just as fast as you can. They're going to cut it down. You holler from the top and tell them to run like hell."

Kay made another visit to the Lovells, specifically to question V.L., only V.L. wasn't home. Politely he knocked on the door, and his wife, Blondean, and daughter Martha answered.

"Ms. Blondean, I hate to do this, but I've been warned," said Bub Kay to V.L.'s wife. "I've got to search your house. I've got word that you've got liquor in your house." He turned to walk the front yard, checking for evidence.

V.L. had brought in a half gallon of liquor earlier in the day to hold for someone to pick up that night. Blondean had just finished baking a cake and the house smelled of sugar. The old gas stove had a pilot light that had to be lit every time the oven was used, and for now, it was off while the cake sat inside the oven, cooling. She grabbed the cake out of the oven, tossed that jar of whiskey in the back, and placed the cake back in the front.

"Ms. Lovell, I've got a warrant to search your house," he said after searching out front.

Blondean walked right up to him and looked him in the yes. "Bub Kay, you can search my house all you want, but if you cause my cake to fall, you're in trouble 'cause it's for church." She stared him straight in the eyes, glaring, never backing down. He turned around and left.

"He and daddy were friends," says Carlos. "Daddy never paid him," but he also claims that you "couldn't do what you done if you didn't pay some of 'em." Bub Kay and David Ayers would come every Christmas and Thanksgiving and get their turkeys and buttermilk. "Those kind of people will never let you down. You be good to them, and they'll be good to you."

Carlos remembers another visit from Bub Kay:

> *I's plowing a horse out in the field, an' old Bub Kay come by driving a 1939 Ford. He asked for Daddy. Daddy got through talking to Bub Kay, and Bub drove on down the road. He told Daddy he was going to fish that creek out tomorrow around twelve o'clock. Daddy told me, "Go get that mule loose from the sled. We gonna run that still till daylight in the morning, and when you leave, take the still with you." Bub was gonna cut that still down.*
>
> *He didn't tell you he was going to cut that down, but he said he was going to fish the creek. Daddy knew. He didn't go to school but he knowed. Just like we's at Chimney Gap one time a foxhunting, and we had a still down there. We saw ol' Bub pull over and sat there a few minutes. He was just telling us he was going to cut it down the next day. We had enough sense to know.*

Bub Kay was "one of the best lawmen that's ever hit this country," remembers Dub. "He'd catch you. Now, if you didn't think he'd catch you, you got another thing coming. He was federal. He was honest and gave everybody a chance to make a living. And don't try to get too big for your britches. He'd see you driving an extra car, he'd say, 'You better leave that stuff alone.'"

Kay and his wife, Louise, were killed in an automobile accident on September 16, 1960, in Cornelia, Georgia. Recalls Dub, "Whoever hit 'em, knocked him so hard, knocked his shoes off his feet. When they buried him, I bet there's over a hundred liquor men behind him, following his casket to the grave."

Most of the Lovell family trusted and counted on the fact that revenuers didn't really want to catch them because if they had wanted to, "they would have caught us. They could have taken us to jail anytime they wanted."

Even after Virgil's death in 1962, they still came.

"We had one come by the house," remembers Judy, "and he had been sent to catch me and Mr. Virge."

She looked at him square in the eyes. "You won't catch me 'cause I don't deal with it anymore, and my daddy's in the ground. I don't think he'll be selling any." She paused and then questioned him. "You didn't catch him, did you?" He, ol' Hugh Merkle, stayed in the house over an hour and a half, stalling while someone searched the barn. When he left, Judy took her mama to the front bedroom and pulled the curtains back from the window.

"Don't do nothing. Don't turn a light on. Just watch. When they get to the persimmon tree, watch for the brake lights." The tree was on the far side of the driveway, some fifty yards from the house. The brake lights went on, and as Judy suspected, they watched a guy jetting from the barn slide into the open door of the car.

"The next morning," continues Judy, "I went out to the barn. I always left my pitchfork where I left it. My fork was moved. I went upstairs, and the hay was pulled out. I just laughed. I thought, 'We won't sell none this weekend. We'll wait awhile.'"

There were forty cases hidden in the barn, all strategically placed by Virgil and Judy, and not one had been discovered.

Chasing Fruit Jars

When it came down to it, federal revenuers chased corn, yeast and sugar—and, in the Lovells' case, fruit jars.

It was August 1961, and Carlos Lovell was thirty-three years old and his brother Fred thirty-two. It was between late summer and early fall in Batesville. The sticky heat of a southern summer was thick and unforgiving. The yield of the spring planting was being gathered, and the corn harvest was plentiful. It was perfect liquor making time. The trees held their leaves, so cover remained. It would be a couple of months before leaves would fall, disclosing concealed shacks on backwoods streams. As far as anyone knew, life was rolling along.

For criminal investigators Billy Moore and Charles W. Hagueley of the Gainesville Alcohol and Tobacco Tax Division, days began early and often didn't end until the dark of night. Their responsibility was uncovering illicit whiskey production, and now, they had been assigned to uncover Habersham County's illegal activity. They were on the trail of Fred and Carlos Lovell. The watch began on August 15.

According to grand jury documents, a still was thought to be across the road from Fred's house, about 8.5 miles from Clarkesville on Highway 197. From August 15 until November 6, Moore and Hagueley surveyed the comings and goings of the brothers, as well as two other primary players and other members of the Lovell family.

Moore issued the following statement:

> *On November 2, 1961, I was at a point about 200 yards north of* [the]
> *residence of Fred Lovell. At about 6:30 p.m., I saw Fred Lovell come from*
> *an illicit distillery in a truck that was loaded with cardboard boxes bearing*
> *the word "Atlas." This truck was driven from the distillery to the garage*
> *of Fred Lovell. The cardboard boxes were unloaded in the frame garage of*
> *Fred Lovell. I am positive that the jars in the boxes were filled with whiskey.*
> *I went to the distillery, and the mash at the distillery was still hot. The*
> *distillery was still hot from being run off. On November 3, 1961, at about*
> *the same time as on November 2, 1961, a blue Chevrolet truck came from*
> *the distillery to the garage of Fred Lovell, and unloaded about 50 cases of*
> *½ gallon glass jar cases. The glass jars were full from the way that they*
> *were unloaded from the truck.*

Hagueley adds that "the truck left the residence of Fred Lovell and was driven in the direction of Clarkesville, Georgia."

On November 6, based on this evidence, a search warrant was issued for the Fred Lovell property.

Once on the scene, the federals arrested Fred.

"The man in charge was rough," remembers Fred. "They had me grab my pocket book and go through everything." A man walked up and questioned his behavior, "The man ain't resisting?" They appeared to cool down at that point, but "they's going to be big boys and bust it [jars] in the yard." Fred told them he didn't want all that glass in his yard. "I'll help pour it out if you'll let us take it." They busted it down at Shoal Creek. "There's [still] glass there," he believes.

Carlos confirmed Fred's angst. "They's gonna break it right there at Fred's house. We had all the liquor at his house, all we could put in that building"—the car shed was full. When the agents inventoried the property, there were 192 cases (1,152 gallons) of whiskey discovered in half-gallon glass jars.

They let him "come down the next morning and make bond."

Fred pleaded not guilty and posted a $500 bond the next day. On October 1, 1962, a six-count indictment, Criminal Case No. 5265, was filed in the U.S. District Court, Gainesville Division, against four defendants: Carlos and Fred Lovell and two others.

Count one laid out the broader charge, one that was rote to most law agencies in the South: "To defraud the United States by manufacturing, distilling, possessing, transporting, removing, depositing and concealing distilled spirits on which a tax is due the United States." Continuing its explanation, the U.S. District Court concluded that "unknown quantities of mash and non-tax-paid whiskey…on or about August 15, 1961 to November 5, 1961; 7596 gallons of mash, 262½ gallons of non-tax-paid whiskey on or about November 5, 1961."

Interest in the Lovells began in late September when a co-conspirator made arrangements to "purchase large quantities of one-half gallon glass jars." On September 29, arrangements were made to transport "161 cases of Atlas half-gallon glass jars from Asheville, North Carolina, to the residence of Carlos Lovell…where the jars were unloaded and placed in the basement." On October 6, 1961, "186 cases of Atlas one-half-gallon glass jars" arrived at the home of Carlos Lovell. Again, in late October, "898 cases of Atlas and Ball one-half-gallon glass jars" were transported from Asheville, North Carolina, but this time, to the river bridge in Clarkesville, where the jars were transferred to a "black stake body truck." On several occasions, Fred and Carlos "transported, removed and concealed an unknown quantity of non-tax-paid whiskey" at Carlos's house, and finally, on November 2, unknown quantities were transported to Fred's residence. This led to the November 6 search and seizure. In total, the Lovell brothers possessed 1,152 gallons of whiskey that day.

Counts two through six further defined the charge in that they had in their possession "distilling apparatus," made and fermented mash, possessed "certain distilled spirits" and "willfully and knowingly work[ed] in a distillery."

A petit jury was named, witnesses gathered and evidence compiled, including several black-and-white photographs missing from archived court documents. Evidence included tag receipts and photographs of a 1954 Chevy and a 1951 Ford. A subpoena was issued for James D. Moorehead of Asheville, North Carolina, in conjunction with the Lovells' purchase of 898 Atlas half-gallon jars, covertly billed to Dick's Hill Grocery in Clarkesville, Georgia. Witnesses included seven ATU agents, including the two arresting investigators, as well as Investigator Cullen Lott, who was the eyes in Asheville, North Carolina.

Both Fred and Carlos waived arraignment and pleaded not guilty to all charges. On October 8, 1962, the trial began. What happened between that date and April 8, 1963, is unavailable in court records, but Fred withdrew his not-guilty plea and entered one of guilty. He was found to be "guilty as charged and convicted," and he was sentenced to two years' probation with final orders to "live a clean, honest and temperate life."

With the case still pending against Carlos, on October 7, 1964, the federal court asked for more information and records concerning a 1961 Ford one-ton truck as well as tag registrations for a black three-quarter-ton flatbed Ford and a 1954 Chevrolet dual-wheel green truck. They also requested original receipts showing sale of multiple cases of Atlas half-gallon glass jars. On October 19, 1964, Carlos was acquitted of all charges and discharged.

After spending five years at this still location, the arrest and seizure ended Lovell liquor production. "It was for a while," laughs Fred.

FOR OLD TIMES' SAKE: A NARRATIVE

It was the end of liquor business for Carlos and Fred. Fred served his probation and then moved seamlessly into his broiler and real estate businesses. Skirting indictment and possible conviction, Carlos did the same, only old habits die hard, and he felt sure he had one more run left in him.

Still living in the Batesville area, he left his familiar stomping grounds moving south into Banks County, where he worked with T.J. Harper, a previous successful partnership. He approached Carlos and asked about whom they could find to make liquor and run a shack.

"It was just me and another guy," he recalls. He went to a local and asked, "Do you wanna make liquor?"

"I ain't gonna work for less than $125 a day," he responded.

"That means you're gonna have to make 125 cases a liquor a day," explained Carlos, promising him only one dollar from each case.

He said he could do it, and they started. "We made 125 cases a day, not one day, but every day."

Cases were sold at twenty dollars each:

> Old sugar liquor, old moonshine liquor. Back in them days, everybody made that ol' sorry liquor. You couldn't sell the good stuff, wouldn't bring no more. Daddy never did. He always said make good liquor. I made plenty of that other. Just liquor. Just makin' it and running it all day long. Say we had run twenty bags of sugar a day, we'd put the sugar on that same ol' slop, and put it right back in the box, same old stuff all the time. Never mashed no meal or nothin'. The good takes a little more time.

By that time, haulers came in by tractor-trailer, backing directly up to the shack. They would unload the truck's sugar load and then reload with about four hundred cases of liquor. Whether they were headed to the farmers' market in Atlanta or to Greenville, haulers showed up at the Banks County pickup as long as the shack produced.

"Lots went straight to Junior Johnson," claims Carlos. "Ninety percent went to him."

Carlos ran for a couple years, but he eventually decided he didn't want to get caught. And that "was the last for me."

VII
A LEGAL RUN

Have to make hay while the sun shines.
—Virge Lovell

Tennessee legend Popcorn Sutton said moonshining was a "hell of a way to make a living." In 2002, he shared his moonshine skills with documentary filmmaker Neal Hutcheson, who filmed Sutton's step-by-step process. The Emmy award-winning documentary *The Last One* included a ride-along with Sutton in his Model A, spouting obscenities and surveying back roads in search of a still site. With water as his priority, he found the spot and then, step by step, erected what he called "one of the best ever," but he swore it was "the last run of likker I'll ever make." Old habits die hard, and in 2008, his Parrottsville, Tennessee home was raided with federal authorities seizing three stills, hundreds of gallons of mash and more than 850 gallons of moonshine stored in an old school bus. He was arrested on three counts of making moonshine and one count "of being a felon in possession of a firearm." With Sutton's four prior convictions, the first dating back to the early 1970s, U.S. district judge Ronnie Greer sentenced Sutton to the optional lesser eighteen-month sentence, for "if 18 months (in prison) doesn't deter you, I don't think 24 months will either," as reported in the *Greenville Sun*. Almost a year to the date of his conviction, rather than report to prison in bad health, he died in his green Ford Fairlane of carbon-monoxide poisoning.

He predicted that "in the next five years, there won't be no moonshine likker." Like his assumption that his poor health would validate the house arrest option rather than imprisonment, he was wrong.

Did You Dress Him?

What are you talking about?

Carlene stood front-and-center at the Southern Wine and Spirits downtown Miami office/warehouse in 2011. She was introducing Ivy Mountain Distillery and their Sour Mash Whiskey to the south Florida salesmen, delivering the legacy of Virgil Lovell and the Florida debut of the Lovell brothers' product. Photographs of Carlos and Fred at work in the distillery, lifelike and impressive, were projected onto screens and most certainly were capturing the attention of the suits in attendance. The presentation completed, she stood back and waited for questions. Hands flew up.

"Did you dress him?"

"Excuse me," she said, unsure of where the conversation was headed. "Daddy's very with it," she replied. She couldn't help but think they assumed that at his age of eighty-three, he was no longer capable of caring for himself, that she must dress and tend to him. "No, Daddy's in good shape."

"Are you telling us that's the way your dad dresses? Khaki pants and a white shirt?"

"Pretty much, that's what he wears," she responded.

"We've watched the moonshine show. We know what kind of life you've had. We know you got him out of those overalls and sweaty shirts. All that drinking and carrying on."

They did not believe her.

Coming Full Circle

A year earlier, in November 2010, Carlene made her weekly three-hour drive from Charlotte, North Carolina, to visit her father. Although not the home she grew up in, Carlos's residence in his development of Mountain Legends Subdivision holds memories and artifacts of her childhood. On the wall in her father's study hangs a small framed portrait of her mother, Ruby, elegantly dressed in burgundy, appearing regal and classic; in contrast, her father's massive portrait hovers in the living room, stern and rigid, appearing to anchor its surroundings of ornate bottles of aged whiskey and an ebony Wurlitzer baby grand. Always there is Barbara Lockwood, a breath of fresh air and stability, who, at seventy-two, is strikingly beautiful and provides a soft edge to this sharp estate. She has cared for the Lovell family since Carlene turned four-years-old, and now, her attention is directed only at Carlos.

"I want to make liquor again." Carlos announced to Carlene with his usual grit.

Shocked was an understatement.

"You can't make liquor again, Daddy," she said in her quiet voice.

Never skipping a beat, he stated he was going to be making liquor legally and her job was to get the licenses.

"I can if you do what I tell you to do. We're gonna put up a still."

That was that.

Carlene always wanted to make her father happy, and this moment was no exception. Having no background in business, Carlene struggled. A former English teacher, she "waded into unknown waters"—the process of licensing and forming a small business from scratch.

After months of interviews and hundreds of submitted forms, Ivy Mountain Distillery was granted a federal license in April 2011. One arduous ordeal behind her, the next hurdle proved to be even tougher: the local license. After the initial plans of constructing the distillery on the Annandale property on Hardman Road in Clarkesville were nixed, Mount Airy issued a go-ahead for the distillery to locate there. Carlos purchased property, and construction began. Once the initial federal license was amended for the final location, they obtained the local license in July 2011 and the federal license in August 2011.

With breweries, wineries and distilleries opening doors daily across the United States, choosing an original name became formidable. They considered Annandale since Annandale Spring was their water source; however, a winery in St. Helena, California, claimed that name, and since they were in the same class, it was off-limits. They debated others and finally decided on Ivy Mountain, a mountain just over the ridge from the Lovell homeplace, and ironically, a mountain, according to Carlos, that never shouldered a Lovell still. It is now trademarked and registered.

All had to be in place—the federal and local license, as well as the physical distillery—before application could be made for the state license. It was a large risk to sink barrels of money into an enterprise before knowing if it could go forward, but as Carlos says, "It's been a risk all my life." The state license was granted in October 2011. Once a Distributor of Record was filed with the federal government, they could start manufacturing.

As for the still, Carlos and Fred connected the dots from long ago, providing technical specifications for Matt Thomason of Angry Iron

Metalworks in Toccoa, Georgia, in its construction and final assembly. The design is similar to what they used in the woods, with the exception of its intent to stay in one location rather than being able to be torn apart at a moment's notice. The science of the system is unchanged.

Building from the ground up, Ivy Mountain Distillery found its manager, distiller or jack-of-all-trades in Mike Yearwood. Other than knowing how much rum to add to his Coke, he knew nothing of liquor or distilling. He didn't know what a still looked like much less what to do with a hydrometer. Sergio Coronilla joined him, and in tandem, both learned how to manufacture the liquor maker's illegal brew the legal way.

It wasn't until his first day on the job that Mike Yearwood met Carlos. All warnings from those who knew the old-timer proved on target: he was a "handful when things weren't moving quickly enough in the right direction." His notion of doing things "right now" became their first stumbling block. "To Carlos, delayed obedience is the same as disobedience," explains Yearwood. "If Carlos says for me to meet him at the spring at 2:00 p.m. to clean it, and I arrive at 2:00 p.m., you can be sure he will already be cleaning it himself." It was a trait drilled into all the Lovell children by their daddy that *now* was the perfect time to complete a task, even if *now* wasn't the time. The process, any process, had to be moving "quickly enough in the right direction" for his thinking, and if not, Yearwood felt the push of the old-timer.

There have always been strict steps to follow and reasons for doing them when distilling whiskey, according to Yearwood. A student of Carlos the first year, he was an observer and a follower, doing nothing more than following the instructions he was given. With time came knowledge and friction. "This caused me a lot of grief," says Yearwood, "as I tried to make changes to the process based on my limited understanding of the process. The most complicated part is that no matter how many times you repeat the process and think you are doing it exactly the same, you learn to expect what you didn't expect." With each day drafting a "sink or swim" mentality, oftentimes the final product would require a throwback to the basic process and a new beginning.

Yearwood admits that every day involves researching the science of distilling. With no background in organic chemistry or prior knowledge of a working distillery, Yearwood is a liquor maker in progress. He has learned the steps, and "because Daddy said so" became more of a blind instruction than an exact science. "I've never followed too closely behind the blind instructions," says Yearwood. "I have always needed to know how and why things work regardless of what I was doing."

He continues, "After three years of the whiskey process and a lot of sprouted malt, ground grain, cooked mash, I am confident of the contribution of each step and how each relates to the other."

There will not be a time when you enter the distillery that Carlos does not speak of Yearwood and Coronilla, mostly sprinkled with haughty sarcasm but always with an underlying layer of praise. All three smile and then go back to business.

"He only had to see it but one time," says Carlos of Yearwood. And of Coronilla, he says, "He's a good un, too."

"I have never had a first batch," explains Mike. "Each next batch is connected to the previous batch and the next batch. It has a lineage."

It was sour mash whiskey from the beginning, Virgil's recipe, and according to Carlos, "You can't make much better than sour mash whiskey."

Contrary to the thought of many, sour mash is not the flavor of the whiskey, but rather a traditional process of distilling. A portion of the old or previous batch, often referred to as "sour" or "spent" mash, is used as the base to the subsequent batch. According to Wikipedia, "The mash—a mixture of grain, malt and water—is conditioned with some amount of spent mash…also known as spent beer. By using an established and known fermented 'sour,' this fermentation process controls the introduction and growth of foreign bacteria and yeasts that could damage the whiskey and improves the consistency and quality of the liquor."

It is for product consistency that "99 percent of American whiskey is sour mash," according to Jack Smith, a certified specialist of spirits in Atlanta, Georgia.

With the recipe alive in only their memories, Carlos and Fred's well-developed palate became the basis from which Yearwood began. "Me and Fred taste it, we all taste it," says Carlos, but there is really no need. "We know what it's going to taste like before we make it." Fred agrees that it's the "same recipe as when we started making liquor."

They always return to the fact that whiskey is meant to sell, not to drink, at least from their perspective. Carlos adds, "If everyone in the country drank as little as I do, we would all go broke."

Since their first run in January 2012, every morning has been the same. Yearwood and Coronilla arrive in the early morning hours. By 6:15 a.m., Carlos has arrived, carrying breakfast for the crew—a habit from the shack days—and he's ready to start.

It's what happens before this moment that makes Ivy Mountain Distillery and the Lovell brothers rare among distillers. The artisan craftsmanship starts with the creation of the malt, for which white and yellow corn is gathered, soaked, spread and ground—all by hand. "That's what makes our whiskey so special," says Carlene. "[It's] that daddy and Fred make it themselves at the spring."

With the farm-to-table movement exploding in kitchens throughout the United States, it is a natural progression to expect the same in the glass.

Melba Newsome writes in *Bon Appétit* that "the moonshine renaissance is both a product of and a boon to the boom of artisanal distillers that have cropped up across the country in recent years." Enter Ivy Mountain Distillery.

Locally sourced ingredients from area farms are fundamental to the Lovells' entire process. From local grains and fruits to fresh spring water, quality elements make up this home-ground creation, and the Lovells never sacrifice steps or ingredients because in the end, those are what can make or break their product's final review with consumers. With the exception of barley malt from Wisconsin (not available locally) and barrels from Jack Daniels in Tennessee, all materials are found nearby in North Georgia, a great source of pride for the Lovells. The barrel corks arrive from Portugal, the only source of quality cork.

Defined as the "water of life," whiskey that comes from a particular region, according to Heather Greene in *Whisk(e)y Distilled,* "often expresses character traits unique to the place, and will depend upon factors such as grain, terroir, whiskey-making methods and equipment, history and even government laws that dictate what sort of label is allowed on a bottle and how the whiskey must be made."

The process of establishing the Lovells' whiskey's character begins at the Annandale spring warehouse.

About twenty-five bushels of local corn are loaded into a spring water–filled stainless steel tank, where the corn remains for about forty hours. Afterward, the corn is bagged and carried to the loft of the warehouse, laid out in a single layer and left for three to four days for sprouting, the natural conversion process.

"Takes about two days to dry," says Fred. "It's just as pretty and white as it can be." Knowing the color it should take, each travels periodically during the day to the spring—some twenty miles from the distillery—to check on the corn's progress. After it is ground, it, along with tankers of spring water, is transported to the distillery.

Eight ferment vats or boxes (each holding 300 gallons of liquid) rest to the right of the 175-gallon copper still that sits tall in the warehouse. If it's Monday, the run is beginning with the mixing of malt and spring water and

Carlos at the springhouse, Hardman Road, Clarkesville. *Seeing Southern.*

At the Annandale warehouse with (left to right) Carlos, Carlene and Fred. Corn is spread in a single layer and left for three days of drying and sprouting. *Seeing Southern.*

the addition of more malt with barley and yeast as the process continues. By Tuesday, the mixture dances as the fermentation process picks up speed. It will take four days of bubbling, adding and resting before the mash is ready; it's a building process, they say.

"Each ferment box is its own batch," says Yearwood. "We run four boxes a day." This adds up to sixteen batches a week at their current production rate. On average, each batch produces the contents of 700- to 750-milliliter bottles at 86 proof with a weekly total of 11,500 bottles, "give or take."

Numbers are important, and for that reason, Yearwood and Coronilla are continually glancing at their watches. Appearing more like precision clock movement than organized chaos, in reality, the process is a developing one that is alive and is affected by "an ever-changing list of variables," according to Yearwood. A distiller's mastery is determined when he encounters those variables, and in the end, he produces a consistent, quality product.

By Friday, the beer, or mash, is ready, and a pump begins the transport process from the boxes—flowing into the pre-heater and then to the still through the thump, the dry thump, the pre-heater and the condenser—right into Carlos's bucket.

Sergio Coronilla changes the still, first venting the steam and then dumping and refilling the still. *Seeing Southern.*

"I'm making white man's liquor," Carlos calls it. "Liquor fit to drink. The kind you want to take home with you and give it to your company."

Ivy Mountain Distillery has already felt growing pains and has expanded the barrel room, which now contains almost one thousand aging barrels. Once orders are placed, according to Yearwood, they pull barrels stored at variations of proof and examine the whiskey's color. They determine how much they have to produce, how much of each barrel to use and how to mix them properly to obtain the desired product. To proof it down, they cut it with fresh spring water. "Taste wise, it will always be the same, but we play with the colors," explains Yearwood. Georgia Sour Mash is bottled at 95 proof, Georgia Sour Mash Whiskey at 86 proof and brandies at 80 proof.

"The longer the better," assures Carlos as he eyes his inventory stacked to the rafters. Their oldest aged product is currently at three years.

"Each barrel is different," explains Yearwood, "with its own taste profile, its own personality. That's where the craft comes in." With each use of the barrel, the end result will vary slightly, with the product getting its best charge on the first fill. According to Fred, "you can take a barrel, you can let it stay for five years. It may not deep charge it as much, but it will still help the liquor going in and out of the wood."

If consistency is the demand, choose the Jim Beams or the Jack Daniels, says Yearwood. The generic taste of Jack Daniels, although good, offers no individualism, no ups and downs. "It's the reason craft beers are so popular; they are unique and offer the consumer a little something different each time. If you want the same thing all the time, buy a Budweiser. We offer uniqueness, and that is our distinction."

Carlos plans on running daily, adding more barrels—that is, "if we're alive." Currently, they are making rye liquor, which is a big seller. "It's got a little different twang," says Carlos, "and every batch, every barrel is different."

The Business of Whiskey

Frustration with the system overwhelms Carlos. "If we could sell our own liquor, we'd be rich. The big fish gotcha killed."

He tells Boyd Stough of Charleston, South Carolina, a fan of Ivy Mountain Distillery whiskey and drop-in visitor to the distillery, that "if you wanted to buy a bottle of liquor today, I can't even sell you one." Habersham native Stough confesses that he had a "fair amount of it growing up," none of it legal and most of it green. "If the gates are open, we're going in," he tells his girlfriend, Eva Black. But if he wants to take a bottle home, he will have to visit the nearest liquor store.

With Georgia being a three-tiered state—from distiller to distributor to retailer—the laws are quite clear as to the path distillers must take in order to get product into the hands of consumers.

According to *Georgia Trend Magazine*, the Georgia Craft Brewers Guild has been leading a grassroots charge to amend the current laws to allow some on-site alcoholic purchases. House Bill 314 and Senate Bill 174 were introduced in the 2013–14 session. Both bills failed to pass. In 2013, a committee recommended that retail locations be allowed to "engage in tastings of malt beverage and wine on licensed premises as permitted by local ordinance or resolution." *Georgia Trend* quotes an interview with John Pinkerton, co-owner and brew master at Moon River Brewing in Savannah, Georgia, who says, "What we're looking for is…responsible modifications to the three-tier system…Most of us don't want to get into the distribution business. The last thing I want to do is to buy a fleet of trucks and to have employees and hire a sales force to go out there and do that work. That's the part that works. That's the part that we value."

Fighting the same uphill battle and echoing their sentiment are craft distillers. With laws on the books since Prohibition, Georgia law prohibits tastings and product sales at distilleries. For the Georgia Distillers Association, this marks its third legislative session attempting to change the antiquated laws and make them more advantageous for distillers as well as for the state. During the 2015 session, the association originally supported HB460, which would have made two sweeping changes for distillers: increasing tasting limits from one to three half-ounce samples per person per day, which would allow for multiple product tastings, and allowing limited sales on site, two bottles per person per day. It, as well as the bills introduced for the past two years, died. According to Jim Harris, president of the Georgia Distillers Association, it was blocked by associations and distributors who fear that this new legislation would jeopardize the current three-tier system—total nonsense according to most brew masters and distillers. "We need them," states Harris.

With the close of the 2015 Georgia legislative session, SB63 passed. Replacing HB460 and other previously failed bills and written to umbrella both brewpubs and distilleries, SB63 allows distillers to provide three half-ounce tastings per person per day, plus a "free" souvenir with a paid distillery tour. Still, retail sales remain illegal. Seeking to look at it positively, Harris regards this as "a crack in the system that will give us an opportunity to fix it in the future."

In the last two years, says Harris, "we have gone from five operating distilleries to sixteen. In 2005, there were forty-six distilleries in the United

States; today, there are five hundred." However, the numbers in Georgia will decrease if laws are not changed. "We have lost three distillers, moving to other states. Three others have been approached by neighboring states." With the strict business and product promotion of whiskey becoming more and more difficult in Georgia, distillers will take their product, plus the millions in taxable revenue and local tourism dollars, elsewhere.

"Georgia is backwards in legislation," says Harris. The state is the last in the South to amend post-Prohibition laws.

Carlene believes that being able to sell products at the distillery or online would be a game changer. "Starting any new business takes time, and the liquor business is especially so. However, with one taste, we have a new consumer. We are not allowed to sell online, so there is much that new legislation could offer the distiller in improved sales."

To her, the problem is this: "You walk into a package store, you know what you want. You don't come to shop." With more opportunities for product promotion, such as on-site sales and generous tastings, customers have opportunities to sample and discover what they like best; ultimately, these conveniences sway consumer purchases the next time they visit their local liquor store.

"We charge nothing for tours now and have no desire to charge visitors in the future," responds Carlene in response to the new law. "We are now allowed to give tastings. Being permitted to sell product on site—even a modest one or two bottles—would be welcomed. Having an interested consumer wishing to purchase and not being free to oblige has been detrimental to Georgia distilleries."

And Harris points out that many visitors to distilleries are not visiting to consume liquor; many are simply interested in experiencing a part of history. As Peine and Schafft reiterate, "The point of owning a quart of moonshine is not necessarily its intoxicating properties, but rather, the possibility of participating in the history, culture, and identity of a place. It speaks of an authenticity even more powerful for its illicit nature."

This issue of sales raises ire among distillers as they view neighboring states raking in revenue for the state and their small businesses. According to the American Distilling Institute, Certified Craft Spirits are "products of an independently owned distillery with maximum annual sales of 52,000 cases where the product is physically distilled and bottled on site." They continue to add distinction to the blender by stating that the distiller must use "traditional and or innovative techniques such as fermenting, distilling, re-distilling, blending, infusing or warehousing to create products with a unique flavor profile."

Fred introduces Ivy Mountain Distillery's Spirit of the Mountains to new consumers at the Old Pal in Athens, Georgia, in July 2014. *Seeing Southern.*

Currently, Ivy Mountain Distillery products are available in Georgia, South Carolina, Florida, Texas, California, New York and New Jersey with licenses in the works for several other states. Its current business plan, according to Carlene, is to concentrate heavily on being Georgia's whiskey, where Ivy Mountain stands alone in the sour mash world. "Even though offerings in other states are good," she says, "they are usually on a small scale. It is our home state where we wish to have a strong presence. We are Georgia's only sour mash whiskey; that, in itself, sets us apart." For Carlos, his business plan is simple: "I want to sell liquor wherever people want to buy it."

When the sour mash whiskey product was launched and branded in Texas as Lovell Brothers rather than Ivy Mountain, the Lovells capitalized on the brothers' history of illegal post-Prohibition production. Fred and Carlos were excited at their reception in Texas, and those who came to the tasting were impressed. "Not one walked off without buying a bottle," says Carlos.

"Developing a brand takes time," Carlene says. "Sales are not where we would like to see them, but the competition with established names is tremendous. However, with one taste, we have a new consumer. In five years, surely the story will be a different one."

"We have been producing this recipe for 150 years with unfavorable legislation," states Yearwood. "Of course, we would love to see more favorable Georgia regulations." But for the Lovell brothers and those who work daily to ensure a quality product filtered with a touch of history, Habersham County will remain home. As Yearwood states, "Why would we do it if we couldn't do it at home?"

Black Cows on Green Grass: A Narrative

"There's nothing prettier than black cows on green grass," Carlos says on our return to Mount Airy and Ivy Mountain Distillery, assuredly a reflection on our day's journey into the past, to Batesville and to things unseen. "That's what Daddy always told me."

It had become clear to Carlos that yesterday was indeed a "different day." The Moonshine Highway leading toward Batesville remains as curvy as it ever was; blacktop can't change its path, only the speed by which you travel. I suspect bootleggers would have liked that improvement. There was Virge Lovell Road, which displayed an official Georgia state road sign, but there was no big white house. The bottomlands no longer produced crops but were overgrown by brush and wayward trees. The slender gravel driveway still curled in the same direction and drifted around a curve toward the single-lane wooden bridge, but it did not lead to a destination of any importance. And yes, the barn still stood, for the moment, held upright by three silos engulfed in briars. There were no dogs barking in their pens out back, no Black Angus cattle grazing on green grass, no rustle of bushes with revenuers squatting in secrecy. It was an altogether different day.

"You've got that right," I respond to Carlos. "Black cows just doing their own thing in a sea of green."

Normalcy returns, and Carlos makes his way back to the foot of the still, taking his spot on his stool, crossing his arms, getting comfortable. The liquor is still running, still flowing, making its natural progression into the bucket. He sits and waits, and like before, it will take six or seven minutes before he moves.

Breaking the rigid silence, he barks directives at Mike and Sergio, who look up for an instant in acknowledgement and then dive back into business. Then, if you listen carefully, melodies of old-fashioned hymns fill the hollow space; Carlos is whistling. Today, I hear "Amazing Grace," and it reminds everyone within earshot that for this moment, he is absent, somewhere in yesterday, remembering, letting the liquor do what it is going to do.

While Carlos sits and waits, Mike is doing the math, gauging the alcohol content. Sergio is at the wheel of the forklift, hoisting boxes and dumping filtered mash into the open container that will be picked up shortly by Carlos's nephew, who will feed the sweet discarded mash to his herd of cattle. Ivy, the tabby cat, wanders between the mash vats and barrels, minding her own business, just as any good moonshiner would do.

Carlos looks up at the activity in his modern shack. "We made a lot of liquor back then, the hard way, too," he says. "We made more than we's making right here. These boys makin' it now, they don't have to sweat. Take a forklift and carry it around. It would take me and Fred to unload a tractor-trailer full of sugar and didn't even have wheels, roll it out the back, take a whole night to carry out 150 bags of sugar."

"Some people wouldn't dream of doin' what I done," he continues. "I ain't braggin', but I done some things that might not been right. Might notta been wrong, but I done it, and it's done. I got by with it, and I made money doing it. Everyone I done business with, if they was alive today, they'd say the same thing. I wasn't ashamed of it then, and I'm not ashamed of it now."

Carlos loves meeting people who love his whiskey almost as much as he loves making it. This image was taken at the Old Pal in Athens, Georgia, in July 2014. *Seeing Southern.*

Both he and Fred admit they were in it for the money, but they also admit that it was pure fun. More fun—and money—than any other job could have offered. And were they happy? "We thought we was," affirms Fred.

"I've never had a job. Still don't want one." Carlos has no idea what he would have done if he "hadn't had liquor."

Like his daddy, who "went in one door and out the other" at school, Carlos chose to anchor his life in those things fundamental to it at its most basic level: working hard, pushing himself and others, building on his Appalachian heritage and upbringing to make it through struggles and poverty. His answers were land, liquor and cattle. "I'm trying to operate like he did."

Virgil's influence at Ivy Mountain Distillery is palpable. That's exactly the way Carlos wants it. With each bottle, he wants customers to live their history, taste their struggles and be a part of resurrecting a product and a craft that was almost lost to time. His recipe is more than fresh spring water and yellow Georgia corn; his "spirit of the mountains" includes pride, honor

Carlos and Mike Yearwood (background) finishing the run. *Seeing Southern.*

and tradition. Each bottle embraces a legacy of toiling and risk, and those ingredients can't be measured or listed on a label. It requires only one sip to realize that this product is a long way from the sugar liquor that Carlos and Fred admittedly made when they had an order to fill and little time to fill it. He, much like his daddy did, has surrounded himself with good people, those he can trust and those who will take care of this business as if it were their own.

It's been another long day, and the run is coming to an end. Carlos remains in position until the last drop has been collected. As Carlene and I walk by, Carlos uncrosses his arms, stands up and walks to pick up the last bucket of the day. He glances at us. Suddenly, rather than gripping the bucket with both hands, he raises a single finger, pointing it directly at Carlene.

"This is your fault." A rare smile wraps around his face. His eyes sparkle, and he releases a chuckle.

"Daddy, how can you tell such a lie?" Carlene responds in her usual soft, reserved voice, knowing that this is one of those moments not many children get to experience. Not many get to be a business partner with a mountain legend, a moonshiner and a liquor maker. And she will hold on to this moment, tightly.

He laughs harder and picks up the bucket, dumping it into the drum. His day is done. Another run is complete. He'll start all over in the morning.

There's no other place he'd rather be.

BIBLIOGRAPHY

Allison, Thomas R. *Moonshine Memories*. Montgomery, AL: New South Books, 2001.

American Distilling Institute. http://distilling.com.

Andrews, Evan. "10 Things You Should Know about Prohibition." History. com. http://www.history.com/news/10-things-you-should-know-about-prohibition/?cmpid=Social_Facebook_HITH_01162015_2.

Ashley, Franklin. "James Dickey: The Art of Poetry No. 20." *Paris Review*. http://www.theparisreview.org/interviews/3741/the-art-of-poetry-no-20-james-dickey.

Atlanta Constitution. "A Chance for Real Prohibition." January 26, 1907.

Bilger, Burkhead. *Moonshine, Monster Catfish, and Other Southern Comforts: Travels in the American South*. London: Arrow Books, 2000.

Bowman, Lee Ann. "Rocky Top: The History Behind the Song." WBIR. com. http://www.wbir.com/story/life/music/2014/08/26/rocky-top-house-of-bryant-songwriting-university-of-tennessee-gatlinburg-inn-marketing/14647827.

BIBLIOGRAPHY

Bragg, Rick. *All Over but the Shoutin'*. New York: Vintage Books, 1997.

Brewers Association. http://www.brewersassociation.org.

Burrison, John A. *Roots for a Region: Southern Folk Culture*. Jackson: University Press of Mississippi, 2007.

Campbell, John C. *The Southern Highlander and His Homeland*. New York: Russell Sage Foundation, 1921. https://archive.org/stream/southernhighlan00campgoog#page/n8/mode/2up.

Carr, Jess. *The Second Oldest Profession: An Informal History of Moonshining in America*. Englewood Cliffs, NJ: Prentice Hall, 1972.

Chapman, David A. "Lamartine Hardman (1856–1937)." New Georgia Encyclopedia. http://www.georgiaencyclopedia.org/articles/government-politics/lamartine-hardman-1856-1937.

Collins, Kaye Carver, Angie Cheek and former Foxfire students, eds. *Foxfire 12: War Stories, Cherokee Traditions, Summer Camps, Square Dancing, Crafts, and More Affairs of Plain Living*. New York: Random House, 2004, 290–302.

Cooksey, Elizabeth B. "Habersham County." New Georgia Encyclopedia. http://www.georgiaencyclopedia.org/articles/counties-cities-neighborhoods/habersham-county.

———. "Rabun County." New Georgia Encyclopedia. http://www.georgiaencyclopedia.org/articles/counties-cities-neighborhoods/rabun-county.

"Craft Certification." American Distilling Institute. http://distilling.com/resources/craft-certification.

Criminal Case No. 5265. General Case Files. United States District Court, Northern District of Georgia, Gainesville Division. National Archives at Atlanta, Morrow, GA.

Dabney, Joseph Earl. *More Mountain Spirits*. Asheville, NC: Bright Mountain Books, 1980.

Bibliography

————. *Mountain Spirits: A Chronicle of Corn Whiskey from King James' Ulster Plantation to America's Appalachians and the Moonshine Life*. New York: Scribner, 1974.

Dell, Giovanna. "ATF Busts Moonshine Still in North Georgia." *Gwinnett Daily Post*, August 4, 2007. www.gwinnettdailypost.com/news/2007/aug/04/atf-busts-moonshine-still-in-north-georgia.

Dewar, Helen. "Modern Trends Killing Moonshine Business." *Washington Post*, September 16, 1974.

Distilled Spirits Council of the United States. www.discus.org.

Durand, Loyal, Jr. "'Mountain Moonshining' in East Tennessee." http://www.jstor.org/stable/211641.

Evans, Mari-Lynn, Robert Santelli and Holly George Warren, eds. *The Appalachians: America's First and Last Frontier*. New York: Random House, 2004.

Fahey, David M. "Temperance Movement." New Georgia Encyclopedia. http://www.georgiaencyclopedia.org/articles/history-archaeology/temperance-movement.

Foxfire. https://www.foxfire.org/index.html.

Franklin News Post. "Moonshining Reputation Built on Long History." http://www.thefranklinnewspost.com/article.cfm?ID=9297.

Garner, Dwight. "'Deliverance': A Dark Heart Still Beating." *New York Times*, August 25, 2008. http://www.nytimes.com/2010/08/25/books/25dickey.html?pagewanted=all&_r=0.

"Georgia's Scenic Highway 197." http://scenic197.com/index.php?option=com_content&view=article&id=63&Itemid=71.

Greene, Heather. *Whisk(e)y Distilled: A Populist Guide to the Water of Life*. New York: Penguin Group, 2014.

Guthrie, Patricia. "Moonshine Poisoning Urban Poor." *Atlanta Journal-Constitution*, September 12, 2003.

BIBLIOGRAPHY

Habersham County Georgia Genealogical Records. 2nd ed. Habersham County Chamber of Commerce, 1969.

Habersham County, Georgia. http://www.habershamga.com.

Harber, Randall H. "The Sun Has Set on Moonshining." *L.A. Herald-Examiner*, March 19, 1973. Charles Kuralt Collection, University of North Carolina, Chapel Hill.

Hatch, Elvin. "The Margins of Civilization: Progressives and Moonshiners in the Late 19th Century Mountain South." *Appalachian Journal* 32, no. 1 (n.d.) JSTOR. http://www.jstor.org/stable/40934376.

Holmes, Dale. "Scenic 197 Moonshine Highway Auction." YouTube. Uploaded March 18, 2010. https://www.youtube.com/watch?v=VwdBZ4A2aNE.

Holmes, William F. "Moonshining and Collective Violence, Georgia, 1889–1895." *Journal of American History* 67 (December 1980): 589–611.

Inscoe, John C. "Race and Racism in the Nineteenth-Century Southern Appalachia: Myths, Realities, and Ambiguities." *Appalachia: Social Context Past and Present*. 4th ed. Edited by Phillip J. Obermiller and Michael E. Maloney. Dubuque, IA: Kendall/Hunt Publishing Co., 1976.

Johnson, Burt. "American Moonshine: The History of Illegal Liquor in the American South." Department of Sociology, University of Minnesota, Minneapolis. https://www.soc.umn.edu/~samaha/bill_of_rights/case%20materials/miller/miller_background.pdf.

Jones, Bill. "Popcorn Sutton Sentenced to 18 Months." *Greenville Sun*. http://www.freerepublic.com/focus/chat/2172458/posts.

Jones, Loyal. *Appalachian Values*. Ashland, KY: Jesse Stuart Foundation, 1994.

"Junior Johnson NASCAR Statistics." Driver Averages. http://www.driveraverages.com/nascar_stats/driver.php?drv_id=1000.

Bibliography

"Kay, R.W. (Bub)." Oconee County, South Carolina Cemetery Index File. http://files.usgwarchives.net/sc/oconee/cemeteries/cifd-22.txt.

Kellner, Esther. *Moonshine: Its History and Folklore.* Indianapolis: Bobbs Merrill Company, 1971.

Kephart, Horace. *Our Southern Highlanders.* New York: Outing Publishing Company, 1918.

"Lamartine Hardman (1856–1937)." New Georgia Encyclopedia. http://www.georgiaencyclopedia.org/articles/government-politics/lamartine-hardman-1856-1937.

The Last One: Moonshine in Appalachia. A film by Neal Hutcheson. SuckerPunchPictures, 2008.

Lehmann-Haupt, Christopher. "Men in Groups." *New York Times*, August 30, 1998. http://www.nytimes.com/books/98/08/30/specials/dickey-deliverance.html,

"Lovell Wikle Resolution." Georgia House of Representatives, SR 214. http://www.legis.ga.gov/Legislation/Archives/19971998/leg/fulltext/sr214.htm.

"Mark of the Potter." www.markofthepotter.com.

McLeod, Harriet. "Distillery to Make South Carolina's First Legal Moonshine." *Reuters*, July 28, 2011. http://www.reuters.com/article/2011/07/28/us-southcarolina-moonshine-idUSTRE76R7ZA20110728.

Midnight Moon. http://www.juniorsmidnightmoon.com.

Miller, Stephen. "Legendary Tennessee Moonshiner Plied His Trade to the End." *Wall Street Journal.* http://www.wsj.com/articles/SB123759972941001681.

Miller, Wilbur R. *Revenuers and Moonshiners: Enforcing Federal Liquor Law in the Mountain South, 1865–1900.* Chapel Hill: University of North Carolina Press, 1991.

BIBLIOGRAPHY

Minnick, Fred. *Whiskey Women: The Untold Story of How Women Saved Bourbon, Scotch and Irish Whiskey.* Lincoln, NE: Potomac Books, 2013.

"Moonshine, Blue Ridge Style." Blue Ridge Institute. http://www. blueridgeinstitute.org/moonshine/index.html.

"National Geographic Moonshine Documentary." *National Geographic.* Published April 29, 2014. https://www.youtube.com/ watch?v=Hhuw7REMnlw.

Nelson, Jack. "Moonshine in Georgia: The Story of a Forty Million Dollar Annual Tax Fraud and a Death-Dealing Poison." Special Collections, Hargrett Library, University of Georgia, 1955. Reprinted from articles appearing in *Atlanta Journal-Constitution.*

Nesbitt, Jim. "Making Georgia Shine." *Chicago Tribune*, April 6, 1986. http:// articles.chicagotribune.com/1986-04-06/features/8601250261_1_ moonshine-car-driver-bill-elliott-first-federal-excise-tax.

Newsome, Melba. "The Moonshine Renaissance." *Bon Appétit,* January 7, 2013. http://www.bonappetit.com/drinks/article/the-moonshine-renaissance.

Oral history interview with Junior Johnson, June 4, 1988. Southern Oral History Program, University of North Carolina, Chapel Hill. http:// docsouth.unc.edu/sohp/C-0053.

Osborne Brothers. "Rocky Top." YouTube. https://www.youtube.com/ watch?v=_n9prNixjbg.

Otto, John Solomon. "'Hillbilly Culture': The Appalachian Mountain Folk in History and Popular Culture." *In Appalachia: Social Context Past and Present.* 4th ed. Edited by Phillip J. Obermiller and Michael E. Maloney. Dubuque, IA: Kendall/Hunt Publishing Co., 1976.

Peine, Emelie K., and Kai A. Schafft. "Moonshine, Mountaineers, and Modernity: Distilling Cultural History in the Southern Appalachian Mountains." *Journal of Appalachian Studies* 18, no. 1/2 (Spring/Fall 2012): 93–112. www.jstor.org/stable/23337709.

BIBLIOGRAPHY

Pierce, Daniel. *Corn from a Jar: Moonshine in the Great Smoky Mountains.* Gatlinburg, TN: Great Smoky Mountains Association, 2013.

———. *Real NASCAR: White Lightning, Red Clay and Big Bill France.* Chapel Hill: University of North Carolina Press, 2010.

Poland, Tom. "Hooch, That High-Spirited Southern Heritage." http://likethedew.com/2011/12/04/hooch-that-high-spirited-southern-heritage.

Quarles, Doris. "Champs Thrive in Ga. Hills." *Independent Newspaper*, 1959.

Rehagen, Tony. "Old Spirits," *Atlanta Magazine*, June 1, 2014. http://www.atlantamagazine.com/great-reads/old-spirits-georgia-moonshine.

Robertson, Cambell. "Yesterday's Moonshiner, Today's Microdistiller." *New York Times*, February 21, 2012. http://www.nytimes.com/2012/02/21/us/popcorn-suttons-whiskey-once-moonshine-is-now-legal.html.

Satterfield, Jamie. "The Law Gets Notorious Moonshiner Popcorn Sutton—Again." http://www.knoxnews.com/news/local-news/law-gets-notorious-moonshiner-popcorn-sutton-aga.

Sawyer, Gordon. *Northeast Georgia: A History.* Mount Pleasant, SC: Arcadia Publishing, 2001.

Seabrook, Charles. "Blue Ridge Mountains." New Georgia Encyclopedia. http://www.georgiaencyclopedia.org/articles/geography-environment/blue-ridge-mountains.

Simo, Christy. "Popping the Cap on Georgia's Craft Brew Industry." *Georgia Trend.* http://www.georgiatrend.com/July-2014/Popping-the-Cap-on-Georgias-Craft-Brew-Industry.

Simonson, Robert. "Moonshine Finds New Craftsmen and Enthusiasts." *New York Times*, May 5, 2010. http://www.nytimes.com/2010/05/05/dining/05white.html?pagewanted=all&_r=0.

BIBLIOGRAPHY

Smith, Morgan. "Alcohol Distribution Laws Bottle Up Options for Consumers and Retailers." http://www.georgiapolicy.org/alcohol-distribution-laws-bottle-up-options-for-consumers-and-retailers.

"Sour Mash." Wikipedia. http://en.wikipedia.org/wiki/Sour_mash.

Stewart, Bruce E. *Blood in the Hills: A History of Violence in the Hills*. Lexington: University Press of Kentucky, 2012.

———. "Distillers and Prohibitionists: Social Conflict and the Rise of Anti-Alcohol Reform in Appalachian North Carolina, 1790–1908." PhD diss., University of Georgia, 2007.

———. "Moonshine." New Georgia Encyclopedia. http://www.georgiaencyclopedia.org/articles/arts-culture/moonshine#Portrayals-of-Moonshiners.

Stiles, Barry, Foxfire Museum curator. Interview. November 18, 2014.

"Tax and Fee Rates." Alcohol and Tobacco Tax and Trade Bureau. http://www.ttb.gov/tax_audit/atftaxes.shtml.

Thompson, Charles D., Jr. *Spirits of Just Men: Mountaineers, Liquor Bosses, and Lawmen in the Moonshine Capital of the World*. Chicago: University of Illinois Press, 2011.

Thompson, Neal. *Driving with the Devil: Southern Moonshine, Detroit Wheels, and the Birth of NASCAR*. New York: Crown Publishers, 2006.

Turner, Carol Law. "White Liquor Legacy." Beechwood Inn. http://www.beechwoodinn.ws/moonshine-in-the-north-georgia-mountains.html.

USA Today. "Prohibition-Era Moonshine Is on the Rise." http://www.usatoday.com/story/money/business/2013/10/14/moonshine-bar-menus/2983957/.

"Virgil Lovell." Ancestry.com. Military records.

Washington Post. "Bootlegging Volume Tops Prohibition Era." August 20, 1951.

BIBLIOGRAPHY

———. "Getting a Drink Down South." July 26, 1908

———. "Moonshine Record Broken." January 19, 1909.

———. "Whisky Taxes." August 27, 1951.

Weems, Charles H. *Agents That Fly: A Breed Apart II.* Tallahassee, FL: Rose Printing Company, 1993.

———. *A Breed Apart.* Tallahassee, FL: Rose Printing Company, 1992.

Whited, Jo, and Stephen Whited. *Habersham County Georgia: A Pictorial History.* Virginia Beach, VA: Donning Company Publishers, 1999.

Wigginton, Ed, ed. "Moonshining as a Fine Art." *The Foxfire Book.* Garden City, NJ: Doubleday, 1972, 301–45.

Wilkinson, Alec. *Moonshine: A Life in Pursuit of White Liquor.* New York: Alfred A. Knopf, 1985.

Williams, John Alexander. *Appalachia: A History.* Chapel Hill: University of North Carolina Press, 2002.

Wilson, Charles Reagan, ed. *The New Encyclopedia of Southern Culture.* Vol. 3, *History.* Chapel Hill: University of North Carolina Press, 2006.

Zainaldin, Jamil S., and John C. Inscoe. "Progressive Era," New Georgia Encyclopedia. http://www.georgiaencyclopedia.org/articles/history-archaeology/progressive-era.

INDEX

A

Annandale 25, 111, 115
Appalachian Mountains 22, 23, 37, 54, 88, 91
Appalachian people 24, 25, 33, 37, 38, 40, 42, 44, 90
Ayers, David 82

B

Banks County 106
Batesville 21, 34, 39, 67, 80
beading oil 64
Black Angus 49, 122
bootleggers 29, 67, 89, 94, 95, 99
bootleg turn 96
Bristol, Martha 80, 101
Brown Derby, the 27
butter money 44, 62

C

Carter, Jimmy 50
Carver, Buck 87
Clarkesville 25, 30, 31
Cocke County 89, 90
community 23

Conspiracy Trial of 1935 90
Cornelia 29, 73
Coronilla, Sergio 117
Criminal Case No. 5265 104, 105
customers 54, 62

D

Dawson County 89, 94
Deliverance 24
Demorest 30
Dip, the 32

F

federals 103
Foxfire Museum 87
foxhounds 47, 84
Franklin County 89, 90, 91

G

Gatlinburg Inn 88
Georgia 53, 54, 119, 122
Georgia Distillers Association 119
Goshen Valley 34, 40
government property 59
Gregg, Homer 61

INDEX

H

Habersham County 30, 49, 56, 58, 62, 100, 103
Hagueley, Charles W. 103
Hardman, Lamartine 25, 32, 53
Harris, Jim 119
Highway 197 29, 32
Holder, Carlene Lovell 12, 76, 78, 79, 110, 116, 120

I

ingredients 59, 64, 68, 69
Ivy Mountain Distillery 19, 21, 111, 113, 117, 121, 124

J

Johnson, Glenn 92, 93
Johnson, Junior 91, 93, 94, 96, 98

K

Kay, Bub 82, 100, 101, 102

L

Lake Burton 35
liquor maker 17, 22, 58, 60, 71, 77, 87, 112, 125
Lovell, Carlos 10, 17, 18, 47, 63, 71, 72, 78, 101, 103, 104, 105, 106, 107, 111, 115, 116, 123, 124, 141
Lovell children 40
Lovell, Dub 50, 51, 58, 73, 102
Lovell, Earl 50, 75
Lovell, Fred 65, 68, 74, 91, 100, 103, 104, 105, 106, 113, 116, 121
Lovell, Lillie Kastner 39, 43, 46, 75
Lovell, Peggy 52
Lovell, R.L. 41
Lovell, Ruby 48, 63
Lovell, Virgil 23, 37, 39, 47, 48, 49, 53, 58, 60, 71, 75, 84, 87, 99, 101, 109

Lovell, V.L. 41, 61, 66, 82, 101
Lovell-Wikle Scenic Highway 51

M

Maddox, Lester 50, 52
Mark of the Potter 34
mash 64
money 72
moonshine 20, 54, 55, 64, 81, 88, 90, 98, 99, 100, 106, 109, 114
Moonshine Highway 28, 122
Moore, Billy 103, 104
Morris, Gary E. 27
Mount Airy 25, 27

N

NASCAR 97
Nora Mill 60

O

Old Pal, the 121, 123

P

Piedmont College 43, 63
Prohibition 53, 55, 119
Providence Church 42
Providence School 73

R

Rabun County 53, 87
Raper, William 26, 34
Rea, Judy Lovell 48, 73, 74, 75, 82, 83, 102
recipe 54, 55, 64, 114
revenuers 24, 65, 81, 89, 92, 93, 100
"Rocky Top" 88

S

SB63 119
Soque River 34, 50
sour mash 57, 113
stereotype 81, 110

still 58, 65
still hands 61, 63, 76
Sutton, Popcorn 90, 109
sweet potato pie 45

T

Tray Mountain 34, 67
turtle 45

V

Vandiver, Ann 49, 75, 76
Virge Lovell Road 51, 122

W

Watts Grist Mill 34, 35, 60
whiskey 113
Wilkes County 89, 91, 99

Y

Yearwood, Mike 112, 116, 122, 124

ABOUT THE AUTHOR

Judith Garrison is a journalist and freelance travel writer as well as the editor of *Georgia Connector* magazine. She has contributed to many publications, including *Deep South Magazine*, *Simply Buckhead* and *US Airways Magazine*, and currently writes a bi-monthly column in *Blue Ridge Country* magazine online; she is also an award-winning photojournalist. She and her husband, Leonard, own Seeing Southern, LLC, which specializes in writing and

Author Judith Garrison with Carlos Lovell at his home in Clarkesville on Highway 197. *Seeing Southern.*

photography projects. She was raised in Clarkesville, Georgia; schooled at the University of Georgia (MEd); and remains a southern lady to the core. She is a member of the Society of American Travel Writers, American Society of Journalists and Authors and Romance Writers of America. After spending many years in the classroom teaching American literature, she escaped and now travels the South with her husband in search of narratives that capture the culture and spirit of an incredible place filled with unforgettable people.